The Truth of the Matter

A Journey to the Heart of Things

First published in 2020 by OrtonRoad Books

16 Salisbury Gardens

Newcastle upon Tyne, NE2 1HP, UK

ISBN 978-1-9993086-2-9

'[Socrates] felt that the big truth he wanted must be visible everywhere, if we knew how to look for it. It was not mere knowledge that we want: only the conscious realising of what is in us. Accepting the jest at his mother's profession, he described his process of questioning as assisting at the birth of truth from the spirits of travail.' (Gilbert Murray, *A History of Ancient Greek Literature*)

'In your last letter, you write that I am a great philosopher. Certainly I am, but I do not want to hear that from you. Call me a truth-seeker, and I'll be content.' (Ludwig Wittgenstein to his sister Helene 1934)

CONTENTS

PREFACE

Universal truth is the lacunae at the heart of philosophy. Its fortunes have waxed and waned broadly in line with metaphysics, which is to say that it is presently rising from the low base it reached four centuries ago. Of course, we are said to live in an age of political untruths. Yet, more generally, we suffer from a surfeit of claims to truth. Everyone claims truth to be on their side. But if truth is to mean anything it has to be universal, indeed primordial. It has to lie beyond human deliberation. This thought takes us into difficult territory, for it seems that the last thing a person will give up is their identity or claim to be a self. Yet, how can we go in search of universal truth if we hold on to our particular point of view? This book invites the reader to see what transpires when they start to think beyond the confines of a self.

INTRODUCTION

The early Greeks realised that human beings struggle to be real, that is just to be. Nearer our time, the claim of one of Sartre's characters that 'we play at being because we're liars from the moment we're born' still has the power to shock. Certainly we can think about what it means to be real and can describe it with a literary flourish. And we can will ourselves into action. But what does it mean to be, beyond just thinking about it or taking action? What does it mean simply to be at one with ourselves and the world? (1) The Greek genius was to realise that human beings require help to make what might otherwise be seen as the most natural of moves – to let go of the self and engage with being on its own terms. They realised that something else is required if we are to be at ease with being real. They called this truth.

It casts a light in every nook and cranny of life. Take friendship. What gets in the way of you and me relating well - but you and me? Me because of the way I let my presuppositions about people obstruct my view of you. You because of the way you *try to be* according to the lights of your 'own' reality. Being is not possible so long as human experience and personal reality sit on it. Only truth will come to the aid of suppressed being. It forever seeks its release. We will address the question of how truth can help humans to relate later.

But first we must ask: where is truth to be found? It cannot be grasped as if it is a thing. It is not material; it has no objective grounding. Indeed, human beings struggle in vain to comprehend it. To claim to do so would be to subscribe to the theory of correspondence between a word and an object which leaves too much of the human and too little of the world in truth. No, the Greeks realised that truth obtains outside the human realm. Democritus sensed this when he said it 'lies hidden in the depth.' But the momentous insight of the Axial Age (c800BC-200AD) was that the inability to connect lies in human beings, that our usual way of thinking stops us being fully human! Only by upgrading thought to a conceptual level can we access truth. A premise was explored that truth is the original pattern (or Form) of being and that in order to make sense of being we need to find its truth. The search for truth came to be the activity we call philosophy.

Truth, Greek thinkers of the Axial Age postulated, doesn't put a single thing to rights. It is not about taking action, making moral judgements or correcting things. But it is about offering human beings a place in an intelligible, harmonious world. Truth helps us understand that we are not individually special, but neither are we set apart or alone. It offers a boon that the notion of self can never confer. Philosophy will continue to offer reminders of truth. Of course we may not heed these reminders, but by merely opening the mind and letting more reality enter we can at least appreciate how tarnished is the allure of life's innumerable distractions from truth.

Even the smallest extrapolation from the work of early Greek truth-seekers opens up astonishing new possibilities. Dichotomies melt away – to possess something can be given the same ontological status as not possessing it. Fixities vanish. The fabric of life may be rumpled but it will never give way. Divisive thoughts, and thereby distress as it is normally understood, disappear.

Truth has traditionally been seen as the rightful place of metaphysics. (2) Yet, it has been suffused with ethical considerations to the extent that it is no longer accessible to us as a concept in its own right. Therefore the full understanding of it requires a suspension of all extraneous connotations towards the realisation that all is truth.

Plato understood truth to be the All that lay behind everything. It integrated the changeable myriad appearances of the Many into the unchanging monist universe of the One. But he never finally took us to the All. He put reality aside as unknowable and instead explored the only vehicle that promised to carry us to it, the mind.

Modernity mounted a full-blown assault on the idea of truth. Post-modernity virtually demolished the very possibility of a universal, sustainable articulation of the concept. If the notion of truth is to survive it has to reveal its hitherto unexplored (or suppressed) dimensions to philosophical scrutiny. It has to be unveiled as a totality that underpins both reality and the mind that contemplates reality. Otherwise we will be left only with truth as a creation of the mind of a self.

The case for seeking truth in the way the Greeks understood it – truth in and of itself - remains compelling. Classical philosophy offers us the insight that being reveals itself fully when we let its unity (the harmonious juxtaposition of its parts) be our lodestar. But first we must accept that unity is obscured by the human disposition to put the self ahead of the world. We fail to see ourselves as the problem because we cannot see beyond a world-view constructed around a self. We use the mind to create heroic or tragic stories about ourselves instead of using it to trigger more and freer thoughts. We assume that a link between humankind and the world must yield itself to analysis and theorising, themselves products of the human mind. Moreover, we remain loyal to a dictum that privileges division, argumentation and particularisation over wholeness. We treat the ideas of harmony and congruity with acute circumspection.

Yet, were we to discover a new concept of truth that opens humankind to the potential that lies beyond the self we will have carried the Platonic enterprise to fulfilment. Ultimately Plato let us down and left truth to others to sort out. Later thinkers, bewitched by a search for knowledge, beauty and moral, ethical or semantic certitude, in their turn failed us. We have always treated truth as par excellence the force that *grounds* all eventualities and intellectual positions. The Greeks challenged us to think about the possibility that truth *dissolves* all positions. The prospect is enticing. A new range of questions beckons. Is it outrageous for example to speculate that something lies beyond both mind and being that might give rise to an expansion of both?

We can pick up where the Greeks left off. They hypothesised that truth-seeking is nothing less than humankind's encounter with being. But my wording here already points to a perplexing aspect of truth – we can search for it but can never find it. We must at the outset accept that we will never grasp the Holy Grail. So I return to the thread that runs through this book – truth-*seeking*. The Greeks understood that the search was a way of bringing all things together in an open mind such that appearances and particularities surrender to the big picture. The mind can be left to fill in the gaps between all the disparate and jarring bits. Truth brings the torn individual being and its relations with others back together again. One can handle all the reality that comes one's way. When human beings live harmoniously they will know themselves well enough to trust their own judgements and welcome the hard-hitting comments of others. Harmony allows people to let go of personal hang-ups, to engage fully in the affairs of the community, to converse easily with strangers and be unafraid to go deeply into, and able to handle the fall-out from, intimate relationships. The classical intellectual call was thus to something universal, congruent, permanent and magnificent and at the same time at the human level to something convivial, conversational, accepting and friendly. When we respond to these calls we can be said to reveal what Plato called the divine in human beings. The concept of autonomy may be the nearest we come to the classical meaning today. But existentialism puts authenticity in the person and it thereby loses its universality.

We have lost much and settled for little. Why for example do people endure lives of desperation? Why submit to the hammer of the superego and become at odds with the universe? Marx said we are all alienated from the world. Freud said we are all alienated from ourselves. Truth-seeking might be directed to the alleviation of this malaise. But this would be to misunderstand truth. It is primordial and therefore has no objective. To search for it in the way we are setting out here is to let go of a purely human perspective: me, you, him, her, them. The viewpoint is universal. This may be why truth has only been approached obliquely for so long. This is not to say that human benefit will not accrue. But to set out with this in mind is to miss the point of the non-human nature of truth. So, the search involves a process of letting go of the self and opening to a universal vantage point. And philosophy never gave up a conviction - even if it was little more than this - that truth and only truth will reintegrate us into the world.

This search was and remains the most difficult task in philosophy. For truth travels under cover and hides behind proxies. It has been seen as God, laws of nature or logic, language, will and life. We must handle its elusiveness with profound respect and not treat a failure to 'capture' truth as a failure of the search. To begin with we are forced to approach obliquely. Strict attention to the imperatives of language and culture holds back the search. By overdoing a drive to comprehend such issues we have produced the philosophical canon. Respect for canonical verities, for unchallenged intellectual structures and terminology, is a barrier to truth. We must face the undeniable - our minds cannot grasp truth. The journey takes us nowhere because truth lies all around. Only when we face all the resistances to this challenge might truth emerge. An acceptance of this awareness has determined the structure of this book. Thus, for the most part my approach will be Socratic, a clearing away of all the mental debris that fills the mind and hinders the making of concepts. Plato discovered the concept of the idea and freed thinking to roam beyond the bounds set by an anthropomorphic approach to things. Stimulated by the Greek initiative I am testing the hypothesis that philosophy is a text that possesses a code more profound than the text itself. Something challenges the text, an energy or impulse. Truth is trying to be born. But it waits for us to be ready to face it.

Homer merely took truth to be the opposite of a lie. But, a few centuries later, philosophy crossed a formidable threshold when it entertained the idea that there is a force we call truth. This force promises to reconnect humankind to being, leaving no problem incapable of resolution and no split unbridgeable. The implication could no longer be ignored that, in the absence of truth-seeking, humankind is a stunted manifestation of being. New questions now came in a flood. Why for example is the potentially rich interplay between being and our thinking about it inhibited by the refractory moves of one of the partners – the mind? Why do human beings settle for the partial truths, degrees of correspondence or connection to being that mind permits? The Greeks realised that, as a first step towards truth, we must educate the mind so that it can release us from a prison of its own making. The last thing mind is capable of, without help, is to know itself. It needs a conduit to the sole thing-in-itself, the ultimate grounding – the world.

It was here that Socrates' great insights and gifts came into their own. He took upon himself the role of conduit. By bringing draughts of reality into his relationship with friends he helped them realise that the mind is a bundle of conflicting positions that begins to fall apart when faced with the implacability the world. Against this bulwark all the pillars of a person's identity are revealed as illusions. In a now-opened-up state mind perforce becomes receptive of swathes of hitherto ignored being. Yet, even at the last, mind refuses to throw its gates fully wide open and let being thoroughly penetrate its structures. It hesitates to allow the juxtaposition of things to make sense. Socrates' conversations exposed the confusion and conflict that results when we cling to positions. Mind and being are kept apart and, when the fulcrum shifts, it is invariably pulled towards the mind. Thus the mind doggedly remains master of a limited self-widening process even as it stirs from its sluggish state. This resistance thwarts the commencement of a dance with being, a dance in which neither is in command, in which the dance becomes all, much grander than either, a dance conducive to the expansion of each. The Greeks realised that this dance promises to generate untold movement capable of opening up daily life to the unexpected and indeterminate. They looked to truth as the key that unlocks the potential of these liberating manoeuvres and sustains the dance.

Philosophy is thus a conduit between people and being. It is not a thing-in-itself; only being is that. Philosophy is the opening up of ideas about this relationship, in Gilles Deleuze and Felix Guattari's words: '...philosophy is the discipline that involves *creating* concepts...that are always new.' But there are limits to the extent philosophy can bridge positions and release movement if the search for truth is ignored. We cannot commence the journey until we let go of the presuppositions we unquestioningly characterise as the workings of our mind; otherwise we can't travel. The carrier of mind is the self, so we must let go of the self in order to journey. But who then is journeying? It is a conundrum. It doesn't matter whether or not this conceptual journey will contribute to actuality: philosophy is not concerned with actualities or outcomes. Indeed, it requires us to transcend them. Human benefits may be deeply enriching, but that is incidental to the journey. So, philosophy invites us to a metaphysical journey. Maybe few will accept the invitation. But it only takes a few to start a discussion, a conversation.

Truth lies hidden, even in philosophy. For Nietzsche it was the will, for Sartre authenticity; today it is often the 'event.' The seemingly bewildering variety of foci owes itself to the apparent elusiveness of primordial or ontological truth. Inevitably we are drawn to ask what it is. But this is to miss the point about its *primordial* nature. It can best be described at this point as a force or process: we can become involved in it, but we cannot pin it down. It is not an object susceptible of knowledge. The underlying question is thus: can we be immersed in being and also think about it as if from the outside at one and the same time? The challenge may be daunting, but the search for truth promises even more than human freedom - it promises a reintegration into the world. What this means at the moment is a conundrum. But this is the Greek message at its starkest. Can we ignore their challenge? If truth arises from the uninhibited engagement of mind with being, so too does the full emergence of the human being.

The Greeks are said to have encountered reality more confidently than other peoples. We today can be said to lean the other way and rarely leave the cave of the mind. Science, AI and binary thinking have come to dominate our discourse; academic philosophy has predominantly adopted a rational, logical and analytic approach. Philosophy has ceded its primacy to science. And yet the focus of philosophy remains crucially different. Where physics looks on the forces that act as fields or planes behind materiality, quanta, black energy and the entanglement of waves and particles as accumulated knowledge, philosophy, which evolved these ideas in embryo 2500 years ago, looks on them as routes to human freedom.

The Greeks warmed to the idea of being or totality, to a nascent metaphysics. They did not attempt to fragment being. A concern with wholeness led them to the idea of truth. But then they realised that the journey to being was led by mind, not truth. So they started to address the way we use mind. This diversion left truth unexplored. This is the legacy of Platonism with which we still struggle. But the Greeks had started on a momentous journey when they set out to clarify what it means to be real. Their first step was to see that human freedom meant to be free from human-centred-ness, from selfhood. The radical nature of this thinking may go some way to explain the long-term neglect of truth. But the Greeks also realised that merely thinking about being would not suffice; that even the Socratic *aporia* or emptying of the mind of social and attitudinal clutter will not alone take us to truth. More being can enter a spacious mind, but what then do we make of it? And is truth a quality or attribute of being or vice versa? What is the truth of being? Is being not fully revealed without truth? Can truth bring all things together in harmony? Goodness once served to hold harmony together but was taken over by ethics. Is truth meant to fill in for goodness? There are so many questions. Nonetheless a search for truth got underway that has never completely faltered. But its focus on a human-centred approach to the world has put inordinate emphasis on the role of the mind. This has blinded us to other possibilities.

The Greek for truth (aletheia) translates as 'not mistaken' or 'something hidden.' These terms point to truth as a core or essence. Free of external influence this essence is closely aligned with being, but it is not of it. It may even lie beyond it. It goes without saying that it lies beyond the structures of mind. One of the few thinkers in modern times to appreciate this Platonic idea is Franz Rosenzweig. His phraseology expresses the complexity of the relationship of truth to reflection (mind) and being when he claimed that 'truth is that alone which is entirely one with reality and no longer separating in it, yet still separates from it as a whole. Truth is enthroned above reality.' (God is truth for Rosenzweig.) (3) Heidegger tells us something similar. His search for primordial truth in Pre-Socratic thinking convinced him that truth emerges in the space between being and an open mind.

Humankind is this space. But truth is self-generating; it is not dormant and waiting to be activated by human intervention. (4)

Even the formidable Greeks seem to have accepted that personal engagement with truth is rare and fleeting. Iris Murdoch summarised their views thus: 'The truth which we can grasp is something quiet, small in extent and to be found only in the lived real moment of direct apprehension...' (5) This seems a let-down, for Plato's invitation was to see truth as the point of connectivity, the ultimate joining up of all the dots, the state of congruity with the universe that human beings lose when they turn away from the world and fall back into themselves. It points up the tenacity of the self. This is the underlying theme in later chapters.

Primordial truth is puzzling because on the one hand it is given - its close association with being means that it has always, already been so, to use Heidegger's phrase - and on the other hand it is approached as if we have lost it. The latter aspect requires of us an intense process of thinking in the present moment that is capable of destroying every shibboleth that stands in the way. Briefly expressed, the process needs the universe and thinking about it. Only philosophical enquiry can accomplish this task: its relentless questioning of all certainties promises a full acknowledgement of the universe. But before this can happen we must remove all that obstructs the flow of thought. This is Socrates's method. His questioning did not seek to reach being as a concept of the universe. This would have put the universe in the area of knowledge, an exercise that science does best. Instead he questioned the mind that controls thinking, the mind that we invoke almost unreservedly as a tool with which to reach the universe. But this consists of structures, filters and feedback loops through which thought has to find a way. An untended mind stops thought roaming the world. Clearing away mind-debris will be my first move.

The hypotheses of wholeness, unity, totality, absolute or reality have of course run through philosophy since Thales said 'all is water.' The formlessness of being did not disturb the Greeks: 'They saw life steadily and saw it whole,' affirmed Matthew Arnold. They appreciated that truth is not accessible via the medium of self, experience or dichotomous thinking; or as a by-product of a search for identity, certainty, stability or the familiar. Highly sophisticated thought systems cannot unlock it. It is not susceptible to theorising, intellectual edifice-building or knowledge-seeking. Indeed, although fascinated by mind, the Greeks were also deeply suspicious of it. It observes itself observing being and knows not what to make of this. It presents being as it sees it, not as it is. We are moved to particularise and thereby to split truth into fragments. But why should we need an opposite (truth and lie) to see a thing or idea? Why settle for truth that changes when circumstances or perspectives change? If truth is a core or essence it cannot be reduced to knowledge or adduced by logic. It does not arise from a reconciliation of relativist and absolutist standpoints, as has been attempted in recent years. Both standpoints look at truth only from a human perspective. (6) When we take up a position we dichotomise being into subjects and objects. But truth raises thought to a 'meta' vantage point above such splits. Now humans relate to being and not to each other. The concept of truth requires a monist environment for a seedbed; it abides in wholeness. Despite all the ironies of his style Plato points strongly in this direction.

This book arose from frustration with the loose ends left by classical thinkers. Postmodernism, similarly dissatisfied with the grand ideas left by the Greeks, has forced us to look at truth again. If we cannot conceptualise truth, if truth doesn't possess ontological status, it says, we still have the fragmented versions that mind offers us, and these come closer to describing the trials and tribulations of daily human life than do remote and imperious absolutes such as goodness, beauty, God - or truth. The classical search for ontological wholeness has got us nowhere. We can instead turn to the epistemological search for knowledge of particularities, to sub-universal truths or truth claims. Following this kind of reasoning, all absolutes have been rejected and truth and being have been left occupying a diminished space. Truth has been relegated from philosophy to science, religion and linguistics. The mind-dominated relation to the world that Plato described closes in ever more tightly. It is in reaction to the impoverishment of a postmodern world-view that lacks both expansiveness and a thorough awareness of beyond-self that I set out on this search.

My aim in the following pages is to find a way to leap (or relax) into congruity, to appreciate that all things join up and everything makes sense. This is a return to source, as Plato understood it. In the first instance it involves returning thought to being. It requires that we let go *lock, stock and barrel* of the mind constructions that have underpinned our social training. I refer to dualistic, particularistic thought, and classificatory systems of thought like Plato's Forms or Aristotle's law of non-contradiction. Only then can we follow the two-step move towards truth evolved by the Greeks. The first step clears away all suppositions in the mind so that thinking is free to roam. This step requires the suspension of

21

the notion of self, the carrier of all mind-constructs. The second step involves the participation with other citizens in the hurly-burly of discussion of every matter under the sun in the public square. Entry into this hurly-burly occurs when one bravely leaps into formlessness; here, paradoxically everything finds its place. Unity is found when formlessness holds no terrors. Observing no longer requires an observer because human beings are both part of the shapeless flux of the world and at the same time are able to reflect upon it. These are the embryonic Greek ideas that run as a theme through this book. As a method I will adopt the Greek conceit of a sculptor chipping away at a block of marble in which the sculpture is latent, waiting to be taken out of concealment.

Section One is an examination of the state of disconnection between thought and being that people constantly endure. Chapter One revisits Plato, where most of these questions were first raised. Plato called philosophers truth-seekers. But what does this mean? Chapter Two opens up the concept of being to test its claim to totality. Chapter Three brings truth out of the shadow cast by a rival claimant. Being and truth now dominate the horizon of our search. Section Two looks at the way humanity loses its moorings in being. It asks what is needed for humanity to accept everything on the world's terms. Chapters Four to Eight illustrate the ways that thinking founders on the reef of self. They offer waymarkers back to being.

Having cleared away the major obstacles to an open, receptive mind I am able in Section Three to see human freedom as the return of thought back into the world. To do this, and to go beyond mere human freedom, I bring to the fore what has been missing so far - conceptualisation - the third and most crucial pillar of the philosophical endeavour. I am now able to watch closely as conceptualisation transforms the relationship between the other two pillars, consciousness and being. Philosophy's ability to liberate thought now makes unexpected things happen. A leap can be made from connection between disparate parts of being to the unity of those parts. The space between a receptive mind and being reveals itself as a hive of possibilities about what might lie beyond both. Chapter Nine takes us into the process whereby ever-larger glimpses of unity can be gained. Finally, in Chapter Ten and the Conclusion I am able to present a radically new concept of truth.

SECTION ONE: BEING AND TRUTH

CHAPTER ONE: PLATO CLEARS THE GROUND

'Plato said that Ideas must be contemplated, but first of all he had to create the concept of an Idea.' Gilles Deleuze and Felix Guattari, *What is Philosophy?*

The Greeks understood that the thought of a thing precedes its being in the world. Indeed Plato said that we can only ever know the idea of a thing, not its appearance. So, we must move from our daily futile attempts to understand appearance to an engagement with the idea. The grandeur of these thoughts is largely lost in our time. They tell us that there are no material or apparent givens in this world. Only when the conceptualising process starts to work its way and the rudiments of a concept are born do the notions of observer and observed make any sense. In this way the Greeks understood something to have arisen from nothing. Entities have to develop into beings; they are not born fully-formed, so to speak. They are not beings simply because they exist or because they can be perceived. Plato was central to this intellectual revolution. His application of these ideas to truth drew attention to its primordial nature and its (as yet unclear) place in the generation of being. He mapped the territory which truth-seeking traverses. But he barely explored truth further. Yet, his point was made: truth is primordial, the source or origin of everything; it *is* being, and might even amount to more than being. And most concretely: truth cannot be accessed by a self.

Accordingly, he laid out a simple two-step programme to move the fulcrum of people's lives from the self to the world. The first step was concerned with personal maturation: it sought to rectify the adverse effects of adopting a self. Socrates asked his interlocutors repeatedly: so you think of yourself as a politician, physician, trader or teacher; why do you identify with this role? I dare you to come out from behind it and reveal yourself. Are you prepared to circumscribe your life with the rules and mores determined by a job description? Is there not much more to you than that which a job or social position says about you? He then proceeded to chip away at aspects of personal identity caused by a zealous adherence to society's priorities. He understood that society's narrow remit takes away fluidity of thought and spontaneity in relationship.

The second step involved the development of ideas. Once personal life was opened up to examination people could participate in the bustle of public intellectual life. The Agora was Athens' intellectual life-blood. Plato illustrated this move by reference to three classes of people attending a sports event. One was the performers; another was the traders selling drinks and food; the last was the spectators. The performers focus on personal achievement. The traders focus on making money. Only the spectators take in the whole event. Plato is showing how a move from focusing on a particularity (performers and traders) to taking a universal vantage point (spectators) allows life to be lived in all its glory. I will use this two-step development as a guide in the process of truth-seeking.

But Plato realised that things go wrong. Even as truth starts to connect consciousness to being, consciousness starts to fragment being. Connection is never complete. Human beings feel swamped by this fragmentation; appearance separates from essence. Fragmentation gives the impression that the world is a minefield of dichotomies - good and bad, right and wrong, you and me -

which we forever have to negotiate. The work of the Pre-Socratics suggested to Plato that the journey towards truth starts where dichotomies originate: in the gap that opens up between mind and being. He bequeathed to philosophy the invaluable insight that truth responds to the conceptualising of this gap.

But he left a number of knots for a truth-seeker to untie. The first arose from his placing conceptualisation in a remote realm somewhere 'out there.' This made truth a hostage to fortune: it was a short step to see the search for truth as directed towards the correct perception of an external and superior being. In so doing he paved the way for an epistemological search for *knowledge of* truth that has beguiled us to this day. Being and conceptualisation were split. Being was not totality.

Secondly, having used so much effort in bringing mind to the fore Plato needed to establish its relationship to reflective (or conceptual) thought, which the Greeks called logos. His recognition of mind was a valid first move, but his expulsion of conceptualisation to a distant realm left humankind with mind (and its propensity to dichotomise) as the only philosophical tool. Plato failed to facilitate the search for truth, but we can see with hindsight that he helped us identify a zealous adherence to mind as the chief enemy of a truth-seeker. Had he taken the step from mind to conceptualisation the grip of self might have been loosened at the birth of philosophy. Instead he left to us the task of reconnecting humankind to conceptualisation.

Thirdly, his concept of goodness is confusing. This concept was a catch-all solution to the dilemma of being. But he incorporated into it the ethics of his mentor Socrates and thereby created fresh problems as he solved others. The idea of goodness is his attempt to bring universal logos into the realm of everyday life. It is God-like; all things derive from it. Yet the ethical definition of goodness is binary: it is the opposite of evil. A binary split was thus introduced at the heart of Plato's logos. It is clear that, in one sense, this is a correct move: the appearance of consciousness introduced a split between thought and the world. Yet Heraclitus told us that logos unites all: it reveals the flip side of binary opposites to be emergent unities. The confusion over goodness lingers in Heidegger's concept of 'in-the-world' and Sartre's concern with ethics as he looks at truth. Neither could let truth become wholly ontological. The result is that truth still occupies an anomalous position - as an intellectual construct, semantic puzzle and as that which validates any claim - all of this while it lacks ontological status.

Fourthly, because of his antipathy to the emotion-rousing proclivities of the poets Plato excluded Homer from his deliberations. As a result postmodernists have had to remind us that philosophy is a second move: it came into a world where mind, language and storytelling were already entrenched. They tell us the Fall has already occurred; nothing is any longer pure or unaffected by mind. There is nothing to do now but interpret the many layers of textual addition that have been laid down since the Fall. Texts are subject to the play of mind, leaving being obstinately distant. Thus we cannot reach back before texts or excavate the original meaning of a text. Philosophy cannot extract itself from the embrace of early poets or narrators like Homer. It becomes difficult (postmodernists say nigh impossible) to liberate philosophy from the all-embracing tentacles of language and narrative.

Finally we must note that an element of mythos remains in Plato's logos. I am thinking of mythos' direction of travel of thought - a human-focused approach to the world. This contributes little to a search for wholeness. At some point the direction must be reversed - the world thinks through and about people - for wholeness to be attained. And Plato never went that far. This book is thus a re-envisioning of Plato's ideas. I am taking it as axiomatic that life is a generative process that depends on philosophy's ability to release mankind's full potential. This is to say that we are not even fully alive up to the point that we start philosophising! Plato reached out to wholeness but was too attached to the mind that thinks about wholeness. It can be expressed allegorically by saying the rays of the sun create everything, but we are distracted by the deflected light from the moon. I take the moon to be mind. Had he let go of the mind (and he may very well have wanted to do this) he would have made being his fulcrum. By surveying ourselves from a place in the open reaches of our thinking where there is space for thoughts to mature, for eventualities to arise, for the realisation that things did not have to arise in the way they did, more being will enter and the mind-being relationship will rebalance. As this happens we become able to be true to ourselves and to conceive of the boundlessness of the world at one and the same time. Only now are we fully alive. I surmise that this is where Plato wanted to take us.

So, at the outset of our search for truth, we have to accept that Plato's attempt to help humankind re-engage with the world has left us with many quandaries. We must start with the problem he encountered, and only partly resolved, that the emergence of thought creates a division between the thinker and the world. I will deal with this in the next chapter. A process that started with the emergence of being created a chain reaction that forced human beings to generate a mind. More being emerged as a result, because mind has the ability to penetrate into being. An immediate outcome was that life was enhanced. But on the other hand dualisms remained. Indeed we must credit Homer with having taken us some of the way along this route. He knew there was an observed world, and that an unobserved world lies behind it. Nature is that which is observed; the gods represent that which is beyond. Then Heraclitus came along and told us these are one and the same. Parmenides' reply would be: yes, indeed all is sameness. He took us further into this sameness, to monism par excellence, to a still, homogenised One. Heraclitus might have replied to this: no, the absolute is turbulent: a fight between opposites characterises the universe.

Today we can ask: why does this difference of interpretation matter? Clearly both are on to something - the nature of reflective thought, conceptualisation or logos. We owe it to the protagonists to reconcile their views. All they are doing is fighting over what 'one' means. They were arguing over the whys of the working of the mind, but didn't realise it. In other words they already possessed a sense of what mind means. Anaxagoras identified it as a force that binds the universe together. But he couldn't say whether it *constitutes* the universe or *obscures* it. In other words, the identification of mind might only have added another element to the mix that is the many. What then is the mind in the great scheme of things? We could apply mind to Heraclitus' thinking and say it causes the war between the many. Similarly we could say to Parmenides that mind creates the one. Reconciling the two successfully was Plato's great project. The 'one-and-many' issue

32

can now be put to rest and attention given to bigger issues, especially to truth.

Plato tried to reach out to people and to reach beyond individual people to reflectivity. It did not work: a dualism emerged from his search for monism. By leaving room in his metaphysics for the dichotomous thinking that can be said to lie at the root of human suffering Plato opened the door for analytic philosophy. Much of today's philosophy will not go beyond the observer. Enquiry stops long before it approaches truth. Instead it gets side-tracked by a fascination with human animation, itself caused by thinking that fragments wholeness. Nonetheless, Plato offered us an invaluable insight - wholeness is a muse that animates our search for truth. The Platonic truth extricates the individual *from* the world in order to give further attention *to* the world. But how can we pick up where he so tantalisingly left off?

Plato managed to hold together a constellation of mutually antagonistic ideas with skill and verve. His mind could engross the most daring concepts. But he was human. Maybe his love of Socrates explains his desire to incorporate virtue ethics into his metaphysics. The outcome is cumbrous and misleading. It is our job is to bring truth to the light as the key unifying force in the universe, a revelation for which he was surely searching.

What can be said with confidence about truth at this point? Quite a lot. It is arrived at by a process of incorporation or appreciation of that which appears opposite to the subjective me, to the other tribe rather than my own, to women (in my case) rather than men. We need not stop there. Rather than standing on one or other side of a divide, we can go beyond both. Indeed, truth pertains to the totality of things; it is universal and absolute. It relates to 'thingness,' to use Heidegger's term. If we are to appreciate this point we must apply thinking to the process of thinking, to the very process that produces dichotomies in the first place. Metaphysics reveals the complementarity or curiosity about what has been left out of the integrity of the world. Only metaphysics enables truth to bridge the mind and the world and to approximate experience to being. Of course, a thought, word, entity or deed must find itself sufficiently close to its object for the two to be deemed congruent or coherent. But moreover, continuity, mostly arrived at by thought, must emerge as a thread connecting a multiplicity of phenomena. This is because truth is not the opposite of non-truth; it relates to being and not to its binary opposite. It rides on a wave of metaphysical thinking without ossifying into an absolutist position. It is beyond human authority, even though it arises between people. It is not already present to be called upon, but human initiative starts a process that sets it free. And further, it relates mind to being, not by bridging them but by discerning unity in the very process of conceptual thought. In this sense it resolves the 'one-and-many' conundrum, because a clear thinker has a sense both of themself (one) and of the world (many). These points are a basis for further exploration, if for the moment they can only serve as waymarkers.

I will use Plato's legacy of ideas as a starting point for the search. But we must pause a moment, because we must be confident that the concepts of being and truth are ontological. This may seem a strange issue to raise at this juncture. But doubts have persisted over both. So I turn first to the thorny issue of being. It is after all the task of truth to harmonise all the parts of being. But does being amount to totality? What does it mean when we say beyond-self, otherness or indeed being?

CHAPTER TWO: WHAT IS BEING?

'If one says accordingly that "Being" is the most universal concept, that cannot mean that it is the clearest or that it needs no further discussion. The concept of "Being" is rather the most obscure of all.' Martin Heidegger, *Basic Writings*.

Plato understood being as a state of mind; in other words, when we think about a thing we bring it into being. Thus being abides only in the realm of ideas. This idea is fine as a first move, but he failed to explain where the thinker stands in this process. How does humankind access this realm when being does not include the one who is thinking about it? In other words, the failure of being to include consciousness means that it is not totality. The 'ontological turn' of the 20th century sought to bring being and consciousness closer together. Heidegger reached back to the Pre-Socratics for ideas that struck a different point of balance on the consciousness-being spectrum to that found in modern times. Modernity's inordinate emphasis on consciousness had cut people adrift from being. But a more dynamic relationship between the two remained elusive. It was left to Deleuze to identify unity as the principle of all diversity in the world. Being and consciousness were now dynamically inter-related. Ontology was no longer concerned with the subject-object divide (thinker on one side; object of thought on the other) but rather with the internal difference of being. The application of the process of conceptualisation to being itself had reintegrated humanity (consciousness) in the world. This is a huge move that we must dwell on.

But first let us step back and see how the problem arose. Before the Axial Age (c800BC-200AD) the sense of totality we call being was hidden. The nearest that human beings could get to it was to suppose a correspondence between thinking about nature and nature itself. Correspondence revealed semblances of being in the form of fate, faith or storytelling. Wisdom amounted to an appreciation of what the idea of correspondence revealed. But the Axial Age wanted everything to be open to enquiry and not just for things to be implied or calibrated. The concept of being or reality was born.

Before this watershed was crossed humankind merely existed. People related to being unreflectively. Life was functional, a tedious thwarting of depravations by nature or rapacious fellow beings, relieved only by listening to stories about life that intensified its colour. Being was, so to speak, the food we eat for survival, as opposed to an understanding of cooking that draws on knowledge of all the nutrients and the ways they interact to create a meal that is more than its constituent parts. In mythos people were a means to an end: they were playthings for the gods, fodder for war and sources for stories of heroism in the myths.

During the Axial Age the power of boundless thought was harnessed on behalf of human fulfilment. The concept of being emerged from the search for wholeness that started when Thales said that all is water. Humankind's place in being was now something to explore further rather than be left unquestioned. Unreflective acceptance of human limitation was challenged; submission to fate was no longer unconditional. Life was not now to be defended against, as if it is always in danger of going horribly wrong or as if others might curtail it. A process beckoned that needed help to unveil. Without intense scrutiny, its subterranean stirrings might escape consciousness. Living became a pursuit of something beyond actuality, functionality or purpose. This wasn't the sense of pursuit we are accustomed to in modern times: a pursuit of power, goods, status, gongs and baubles, and celebrity. Nor was it a pursuit of variety in itself, a search for ever-finer degrees of difference that can block out a sense of impending sameness. These are chimeras; vanity of vanities as the Book tells us.

The philosophical concept of pursuit took a thinker beyond knowing the thing ostensibly pursued towards the very idea of pursuit itself. This is philosophical method at work. Socrates realised that human beings relate well enough to being when they stop guarding against it. Being just is. It is not resistant or problematic; it doesn't need to do anything. Socrates identified the usual ways that people think about being as the chief obstacle to an appreciation of totality. Practical thinking that tells us when the No 8 bus arrives is not adequate to the conceptual task of relating to being. The wisdom Socrates sought involved thinking about the very process of thought.

The aim was to release being from the bondage of unreflective human thought. A reversal of the usual direction of thought became possible. Now, instead of a pursuer chasing after the pursued, it was possible to conceive of the pursuit preceding the pursuer. The pursuit already exists as an idea before it is enacted. In other words, being calls out to us; humankind is not the primum mobile. Of course, this realisation was a direct threat to the self, the apparent pursuer. And yet the more the pursuit itself is foregrounded the more something else happens - thought replaces both the pursuer and the pursued. Thinker and object disappear. Neither is 'necessary' for a pursuit to take place. Energy moves through the universe without there being a need for humans to generate or direct it towards an end. The pursuit can now be reconfigured as substantial and the pursuer and pursued reconfigured as abstractions, the opposite of general usage. The Greek aim of rescuing us from ourselves was thereby achieved. Terms that are generated by dichotomous thinking are seen to be properties of their opposites. Evil is now seen to be a property of goodness. This jump appears too big for the self to make and it beats a retreat.

This is how the Greeks realised that being is a state of mind. The key factor affecting our connection to being is the quality of thinking we bring to bear on it. In other words, we are born into the world only as existents or 'livers,' the outcome of biology. But being is much more than existing or living. Heidegger realised that Plato had left us a problem by placing conceptualisation (logos) unattainably in the outer reaches of the mental world. This made it difficult for human beings to upgrade their lives from existence to being. By 'detaching' the conceptualising mind Plato elevated it to a position to observe being. But this move created a dichotomy at the heart of ontology. The thinking observer looked out on an 'objective' world. (Analytic philosophy still holds to this view.) We are left trapped in a hall of mirrors, grappling with layer upon layer of appearance. We can make claims about the objectivity of other things but can never (without mediation) connect to them.

Heraclitus resolved the problem of dichotomies by conceiving of them as emergent unities. In the midst of flux he discerned oneness. The world was intelligible to a mind able to conceptualise. When we think *about* our thinking we can assume a vantage point where opposites are revealed as exercises that merely separate the apparent from the hidden. When we start with a hypothesis of wholeness the visible can be seen as a property of the invisible and badness as a property of goodness. This distinction applies to truth: it is an absolute and truthfulness is a property of it. The journey from living/existing to being can now be construed as involving two moves. The first one - aporia - opens the mind. The second move uses the uncluttered mind to return binary opposites to wholeness by raising concepts to meta-concepts. Heraclitus used a formula to explain the move from existence to being: 1.) Things exist; 2.) they do not (opposite); they become (transition); they are (being). Attempts to define an objective world from the vantage point of an observer, by reference for example to Descartes's Cogito, only go as far as the first two stages. They do not go beyond the typical opening gambit we make as we open our eyes to the world and perceive us as here and being out there.

The difference between existing and being is affected by the way the term 'Cogito' is translated. When translated as 'I think' it refers to the first, unreflective level of cogitation. When translated as 'I conceive' it means to think about the nature of thinking, or to philosophise. In the latter case we can be said to have acquired consciousness, as a step towards being. To become a being an unreflective individual must first free their intellectual powers of all ties to a mentality or given state of consciousness as found in a family, profession, culture or religion. Conceptualisation can then uncover what is hidden or presently not known and begin the move to totality. Now consciousness responds to being by taking aspects of it and conceptualising them. It matters not whether one

39

takes it that ideas create the world or the world creates ideas but that the responsiveness of each to the other is not held back. Conceptualisation is a third force between consciousness and being that is capable of sustaining and augmenting the fluidity in their relationship. Conceptualising brings things *into* being.

However this thinking came under attack in the 20th century. Heidegger's 'ontological turn' rescued being from the malaise it had sunk into since Descartes' Cogito had brought the self back to the fore. But he only went so far. His first move was to construe consciousness as flux. His second was to search for the reality behind the flux. These were valid moves. To understand appearances as flux and that which underpins them - being, nature or reality - as unchanging is a Platonic move. But, the separation that Heidegger retained between them owed much to Descartes. For more than 2500 years it has been held to be irrefutable that being obeys laws while consciousness does not, and that thereby the difference between them is unbridgeable. But then Deleuze changed the very ground of the discussion by suggesting that *both* are subject to overarching laws.

Heidegger's 'ontological turn' fell short. Nietzsche had already dismissed being as an airy idea because of its inability to critique itself. Postmodernism is acutely aware that the idea of being fails to include the consciousness that thinks about it. It appears to be impossible to remove the thinking subject from the picture.

That is, until Deleuze incorporated into being the issues thrown up by the bifurcating disposition of the mind. He starts from the moment we look out at reality in all its multiplicity, realise we are not part of it in any clear sense, and become confused. We seek to bring everything together in harmony again and are immediately faced by the 'one and many' conundrum. As I begin to think about this situation and try to place myself in it, the many in the one becomes me, and the one in the many is me in the world. This is the point at which the one appears to be scared of its members, of the many. Heraclitus resolved this dilemma by assuming the one *should* accept the many, that the tension between the many should not be seen as a threat to the one. The one should have a sense of its own unity (or the harmony of totality) despite all the differences that emerge among the many. Logos comes to the rescue because it recognises differences, even if Plato's Forms downplayed them. The fact that at the outset all people are different and do not accommodate to each other is not a problem. The one will expand to accommodate all differences. This is a serious challenge to the modern concern with equality. The many need not be equal, because the one can embrace all.

A way of placing being in the human realm is to follow the three moves made by classical thought. The first is to 'know thyself.' This is the area of personal character that Socrates explored in his interlocutor. It involves shedding the overlay of attitudes and principles that give a person a sense of self and identity; they amount to a prison of social conformity. In this way the 'one' of the 'one and many' conundrum is brought into the light. The second move takes the one out into the world of the many to find where the one fits in. Having worked through the maturation of its 'interior' life, an entity now starts to relate to other self-knowing entities. Narcissism and subjectivity are left behind and the one faces a world of otherness and inter-subjectivity. Truth is the third move; it involves us in going all the way to reality. It allows us to accept all the infringements of rules and roles because they are responses to binary thinking.

41

Deleuze's idea of 'the socio'or 'social' takes these ideas further. It seeks to reconcile the interaction of the flux of thought with the placidity and opacity of being. He used this idea to signify a force that penetrates all aspects of our lives. It makes room at the heart of totality for the mental sensibilities of humankind. In other words, it allows consciousness to dance with being. It can claim to be universal and absolute. There is something about it that is pre-mind, pre-logos. Astonishingly, its all-inclusivity gives it a claim to totality that being lacks. It is more than an abstraction; rather, it is a claim to first principles. It is so powerful that it controls mind. Mind is its intellectual engine; it operates through mind's structures and precepts. Its ability to incorporate humanity into being forces us to ask searching questions of ontology.

It can be argued that philosophers have always had a sense of the socio. It manifests in Plato's distrust of mass society in the *Republic* and *Laws*. It is Aristotle's mean, the Hellenists' One, Spinoza's conatus, Hegel's dialectic, Heidegger's Das Man and Lacan's Big Other and Symbolic Order.

The Platonic project failed to alert us to the way mind obstructs the emergence of truth. We have hesitated to look for it in the arena of ontology ever since. Indeed the mind is only the third move behind reality; the socio is the second. Yet all attempts to address it so far have retained strong traces of mind and epistemology that confound the search. The socio is an idea of totality we can confidently take as our base.

Now we can go further. The socio tells us that being manifests as an issue of aggregation. We can take a single organism to be both divisible and indivisible at the same time. When two people meet they slip into a monolithic relationship as if they are both indivisible. Yet, at the same time, they are each internally divided. Thus, when two people meet they see themselves in the other and *at the same time* see a stranger. This is disconcerting. Who are they? But especially disconcerting - who am I?

When a couple stop dancing the ground between them no longer opens to the wonder of more being. Out of a state of perplexity laced with fear each person has settled on a fixed view of the other. The nature of the relationship is circumscribed and new possibilities foreclosed. There is something in this foreclosure that speaks volumes about human suffering. Something is attributed to being in the person of the other that is unbearable. This state of being is what the socio addresses.

It asks the question: How can we get apparent opposites to relate? Aggregation is an answer to problems thrown up by dichotomised thinking. The socio builds on Heraclitus idea that opposites are not mutually exclusive. Aggregation presents us with a non-logical relationship between apparent opposites that can lead to union between them or to the generation of a meta-concept that will embrace both sides of the divide. The move is towards difference and away from division. It challenges a belief that other minds are different from one's own. It is between and within aggregates that energy arises. A state of flux occupies the interstices. This is where conceptualisation comes into its own because the socio can be seen as an opportunity or as a problem. Aggregated minds can replace mind with either being or a disconcerting blurriness. The outcome depends on the quality of thinking we bring to bear on aggregation.

Things change when we approach the issue of aggregation by assuming that others respond to the world in similar ways to us.

43

We can also assume they will possess some sense of our responses even before we are conscious of making them. Now the intimacy of the relationship breaks down the illusion of a split between people. By opening to being through the other we are now able to observe without being an observer, subject, or narcissist. Metaphysics is grounded in relationship.

The socio points to a hiatus at the heart of ontology. Being tells us things are as they are. It is an attempt to live towards truth in terms of the is-ness of things. But its earlier formulation did not take account of humanity's concern with the utility of life. The socio on the other hand incorporates humankind and its preoccupations and struggles and also tells us that people are as they are. It tells us we are not alone. It acts as a bridge between human sensibilities and what Heidegger calls the 'thingness' of nature. It posits a relationship between consciousness and being in which 'us' replaces 'is' in a space expanded to make room for humanity.

Deleuze created a space for humankind (consciousness) at the core of ontology. Axial Age thinkers had taken humankind to be distinguished from other creatures by possessing a mind. Indeed at the heart of Hegel's ontology consciousness seeks to understand itself. But the Deleuzian move reveals human beings and nature to have a common root. Ontology's core is no longer a zero sum game that leaves the two titans of being and humankind (nature and consciousness) fighting over a definable space. Deleuze brought them onto a ground where the movement between them is the key issue, rather than the scale or integrity of each. He was now able to apply physics' laws regarding the behaviour of atoms to them. The locus of movement and energy now lay *between* entities and this energy determined their placing *vis a vis* each other.

In an acknowledgement of Plato's dictum that truth is prototypical or the ultimate concept, Deleuze saw that *conceptualisation* makes sense of the place of all things in the world. The internal integrity of a thing is no longer a matter of prime consideration. He also applied this idea to language: philosophy changes words into terms that are amenable to infinite production of ideas, upgrading them from concept to meta-concept without end. Logos it must be remembered is the root of the term ontology; indeed, the word logos derives from the Greek word 'to lay.' The locus of connection moves from the self to the in-between in the form of a conversation.

The socio creates space for the emergence of wholeness out of fragmentation. It tells us that humankind never abandoned its roots in being; it didn't volunteer itself to be ambushed by mind. Rather, consciousness can be used to *understand* being, not to *compete* with it; to dance with it, not to endure a stand-off. Truth is a method that works its way towards the *knowing* of being; it does not *describe* being's content. It arises as ideas continue to germinate, in the very flux or process of germination. Truth helps us make sense of the relation of being to consciousness as a generative encounter.

Unity is not human; nor is it inherent in things. The generative move that is required occurs only when human deliberation abates. At the moment we are still deep in the exercise of clearing-away obstacles to enable it to operate. We are always in danger of refusing to notice how our thinking fractures totality. In other words, truth is intimately tied to the nature of our thinking: it responds only to reflection, philosophy or metaphysics (which I take to mean the same thing). We have to do more than open our minds to the external world. We have to open our minds to the world that includes our thinking within it.

The socio is a reinterpretation of the monism implicit in classical thought. It is faithful to Plato's commitment to know more about connection. But it has had to struggle with modernity's penchant for prioritising human beings above all things. We must never forget that the first unreflective move of the mind is to place the world outside us. But the socio tells us something more. Its embrace of consciousness or mind (qua human beings) and being or nature removes the last great dichotomy at the heart of ontology. Heidegger couldn't reach this point because he wanted human beings to occupy a subjective zone he calls 'authenticity' and existentialism wanted to hold on to human responsibility. Humankind has remained separate in some degree from being. But the socio tells us that people never left the world. Rather, our thinking 'expelled' us. The socio finds room for human beings at the centre of all things without a diminishment of being. The socio 'ontologises' humanity.

The Big Bang created multiplicity out of singularity. This produced a conjunction of being and consciousness that has tested human understanding ever since. The riddle of how entities (such as human beings) interact within a field of multiplicity arises because human beings are drawn to others in a search for love, inspiration and comfort, for a challenge and a sense of belonging. Yet the Heraclitus-Parmenides 'dialogue' helps us understand what to do when we get there. This dialogue makes clear that movement or flux can rest *within* permanence or oneness. The very *process* of change can be seen as a *constant*. This is a move towards totality; the parts constantly reassemble and tessellate. Now we can appreciate that that which disappears is still here in another 'place.' It only appears to have fallen 'out of place.' The Parmenidean 'place' is out there and the emerging Heraclitean 'thing' is searching for a place in it among all other things.

The idea of being (qua the socio) now stands for totality. So, if aporia was the method that addressed the stasis to which our minds succumb, the idea of the socio resolves the problem of totality that has been fractured by the workings of the mind. The socio tells us that we can stop struggling with being because we and it come from the same place.

48

CHAPTER THREE: RELEASING TRUTH FROM BONDAGE

'Goodness, growing to its pleurisy,/ Dies in his own too-much.'
Shakespeare, *Hamlet*

We must now look at Plato's view of truth. Is it capable of carrying being to unity. Can it relate flux to oneness in a way that does not jar? Plato sidestepped these questions at the outset by only granting truth a subsidiary role in the harmonisation of being. He accepted the classical view that goodness was best suited to this task. We must step back for a moment to introduce harmony. It is an idea that presupposes that everyone and everything can find a rightful place in the world; and that no one will struggle to understand any other. The early Greeks believed harmony arose in the hurly-burly of life in the Agora or public square. Here people could escape the smothering rules and roles imposed in the domestic household and could breathe in fresh draughts of reality. The rumbustious encounters offered by the public square rattled the prison bars of the ego. Relations that might otherwise have been tainted by inertia, suspicion or dislike were open to intellectual challenge and to new depths of mutual understanding.

However, an unexamined life can freeze differences between people into virtually insurmountable, hard-and-fast divisions. At this point ethical ideas like goodness appear to offer a particularly clear path to harmony. Indeed, Plato adopted the contemporary view that goodness would loosen the grip of the self. (1) He made use of the pre-logos notion of harmony (the trinity of goodness, beauty and truth, with goodness at its head) in *The Republic*:

'In the world of knowledge the Form of the good is perceived last and with difficulty, but when it is seen it must be inferred that it is the cause of all things, producing in the visible world light and the lord of light, and being itself lord of the intelligible world and the giver of truth and reason...'

We can now see that Plato's adherence to the idea of goodness led him and us astray. Even a cursory view shows the concept to be overloaded. On closer examination we can begin to see why. Plato was asking goodness to connect human beings to logos, the intelligible guiding principle of the universe, and to connect human beings to each other, at one and the same time. This is impossible: goodness cannot conclusively meet these demands and engross all. The complex and contradictory nature of Plato's goodness collapses as we look at it. The time has come to demolish its status at the head of the hierarchy of forms and finally to return truth to its throne. Conceptualisation or logos connects humankind to being in association with truth. Goodness's failure to harness conceptualisation disqualifies it.

I offer four reasons why Plato's goodness falls short. Firstly, full engagement with being or otherness requires a person to make two moves, both of which are beyond the capacity of goodness. The first move is to know oneself, a question of interiority. This move encourages a process of maturation that can be expected to resolve internal contradictions. Only from this point can a person conceive of the possibility of otherness. Indeed, only now can two or more (by now, self-*knowing*) people start to converse. Goodness might help us understand the content of an encounter (mores, injunctions, rights and wrongs) between two entities, but not the process that underlies it.

The second move can only be made once the first is accomplished. It involves the recognition that the degree to which we can easefully negotiate our daily lives depends on the extent to which we can understand the implications of the 'One and Many' conundrum. Only a relaxed and thoughtful person (the One) can relate to others (the Many) without fear or favour. Thus this two-step development tells us that harmony emerges only when we are relaxed about the way being presents itself. It also tells us that the self nullifies this move. It will be remembered that the Greeks reasoned that the world created us and not us it. We are objects in this sense, not subjects. Thus a reversal of the binary divide is the first move towards harmony. But the self's failure to handle internal agitation obstructs its unflinching and un-judgmental acceptance of the world. The Greeks gave being primacy over every construct of the mind and its expression, the self. Yet, fatally for Plato's project, goodness retains a trace of mind and thereby of subjectivity.

The result is that goodness fails to handle porous boundaries. The concept is only capable of exploring what it means to be an entity. It cannot face differences in or between other entities. People are different and yet moral codes do not allow for this. Certainly an entity is full and sufficient unto itself. It is capable of external movement and can dialogue with another entity. But it is not self-knowing in the way I have described. Internal maturation has not occurred. Its inability to reach inward and find harmony between its internal parts means that when it reaches outward it balks at all the difference it encounters. It treats differences as divisions that have to be overcome. Goodness fails to take the first step of internal maturation, thus inevitably making a botched job of the second. It cannot connect us easefully to the world.

The Greeks had already pondered the question of how a human being can relate to the world. They sensed that the search for the whole, for otherness, or being, takes us to the in-between, to inter-entity - and that only truth can do this. Only a fully worked-through entity or person (step one) can engage with the all or totality of the world such that (step two) they can easefully recognise and accept the differences between and within all other entities or persons. Only truth allows us to accept all differences – to incorporate deviancy within the normal Bell Curve - and moreover not be perturbed by infringements of normality's rules. This is because truth rises above dichotomies. Differences between people are not turned into divisions. Truth breaks down boundaries to reveal the in-between whereas goodness builds boundaries around itself such that engagement with another has to negotiate a maze of rules and injunctions. Truth operates in a monist realm; goodness cannot leave behind its origin in the binary realm of mythos.

The second criticism of the concept of goodness applies to its internal contradictions. Plato treated the harmony bequeathed him from mythos as having three elements - engagement (goodness); appreciation (beauty); and realisation (truth) that, taken together, led to an awareness that being just is. The Platonic good denotes the ways human beings function or comport themselves in the world. However, this concept tries to force together two incompatible statements. Firstly, the good is a God-like totality in which everything else partakes. Secondly, it represents human connection to logos, the attempt of the mind to make sense of things. Some truth must subsist in goodness otherwise it would have no basis in is-ness. Nevertheless, goodness as a God-like totality creates innumerable dualities: for example, the flip-side of good is evil. It cannot relate to logos, which is a universal force possessing no internal contradictions. Plato's desire to include all issues within the one concept is understandable. He wanted the good both to be a connection between people on this earth and a way to connect them to the logos that attempts to make sense of things. Goodness 'has a kind of unity,' according to Iris Murdoch. But, logos cannot possess internal distinctions; it is universal, not a construct of mind. On the one hand, *unless something is done about it*, the emergence of thought (logos) creates binary splits between the viewer and the object viewed. Only conceptualisation can carry us this far. But the ethical aspects of the good, which *are* mind constructs, add to the binary effect of the emergence of thought to make the use of goodness unviable. Goodness cannot claim ontological status. Something else is required that can handle the binary split between the viewer and the viewed object if we are to begin to access being. A more philosophically inclusive and expansive concept than goodness is required.

The third reason for goodness' inadequacy is that it is an unfinished move from mythos to logos. Even were we to struggle with the good, its most glaring omission - the absence of room for potential to emerge beyond is-ness - means that it cannot achieve primordial status. It cannot take us all the way to an expansive being. Plato clearly put things in the wrong place. His creation of a stark opposition between goodness and wrongness has prevented us from asking crucial metaphysical questions. For example, a lie can be seen as a narrative that covers the truth. Leave it alone and it'll collapse into truth. Moreover, the inclusive nature that Plato attributed to goodness (carrying wrongness within itself) has turned goodness into an inherently unreliable and potentially dualistic notion.

Fourthly, Plato's privileging of goodness presupposes we need more of it. But the world does not lack for goodness. The trouble is that we do not understand goodness. It is ironic that everyone seems to know or have values that underpin their actions - to care for the weak, old and young - and would claim that their actions are far from being unexamined or are merely a response to sentiment or appearance. Yet ethics is an enquiry into how to do good without actually understanding the idea. For goodness taken to excess can do great harm. Shakespeare says as such in the quotation at the head of this chapter. For example it may seem ethically obvious to give to charity, and yet charity might indirectly cause the problems it claims to alleviate. Socrates saw that what ethics defines as bad is an expression of that which is lacking or unacknowledged in what ethics defines as good. Socrates' view would allow for the idea that a criminal is one who is super-good.

We must accept that Plato's choice of goodness was not well founded. It cannot stop us becoming fixated on the specialness of our ego-driven selves. This verdict also applies to beauty, Plato's third ontology. Beauty invites us to our feelings. We can share them and realise we are not alone; thus we can comprehend the world in the light of our connectedness. Beauty moreover helps us bypass the view of the human subject and appreciate what is in the world as seen from the point of the universe. It can thereby transform the human observer at the same time as it releases the world. We often lack confidence in our intrinsic beauty. We must first it seems see it elsewhere, in a person, painting, landscape, and so on. Then we can be incorporated into beauty, that is to say, into being that lies beyond the self. If I look at a painting long enough, let go of my ego-driven perspective and let the painting thoroughly come over to me, it will come into its fullness before my eyes. The painting has the power to transform me in return.

Beauty has a claim to be ontological. And yet again: there is a problem about beauty akin to that of the complicity of goodness with ethics. Beauty starts from the human point of view. At its essence is narcissism. It is enclosed in itself, a closed system. The 'I' is within the entity; it is concerned with self-contemplation. When beauty is said to be in the eye of the beholder it turns the painting into an object of the subjective gaze. We remember the critics' opinions, our social training in taste and fashion, and we lose the connection to being. This suspicion always floats above beauty, making it an unreliable connection.

Truth's claim to be the only ontology is incontestable. It shows us that our place in the whole involves a move away from isolated entities to the space in between, to inter-entity or inter-subjectivity. This space assumes a paramount importance that only truth can address. Goodness's place at the head of the trinity owes itself to Plato's loyalty to Socrates. The presence of virtue in goodness creates a conflicted idea that has paraded as metaphysics. The dualism implicit in goodness warrants its wholesale relegation to ethics. This move now releases metaphysics from the grip of ethics to become wholly about ontology. And in this move truth is revealed as the prime ontology.

It has to be remembered that the early Greeks were still attracted by mythos. The call of metaphysics was only just being heeded. The Greeks were drawn to harmony as an aesthetic concept: it aggregates but it also pleases. It only takes us so far because it lacks the boundlessness of metaphysics. But where mythos placed goodness atop harmony, logos was beginning to replace goodness with truth, and harmony with is-ness. Plato had found goodness and beauty to be workable ideas or entities. Nonetheless he also understood the whole to manifest *between* entities. But the intensity of his love for Socrates seems to have smothered this insight, leaving goodness, beauty and truth in a forced union. Our task must therefore be to disaggregate them and set truth free. Only then can we begin a process that lets all entities find their rightful place from which to relate independently to others. The concept of harmony helps us think about the relation of the parts to the whole, in short, to think in terms of difference. Difference calls out for us to *receive* more being, but it doesn't call out to us to impose ourselves on it or know more about it. Difference doesn't disturb the connectivity within the parts of the whole. Plato's thinking tells us there is no gap between mind and being; that nothing intrinsic has happened. Language and the Fall are manufactured phenomena. Yet something prior to reflection has certainly happened, such as an up-rush of love that released more being. So he was able to bridge the assumed gap between mind and being by falsifying dichotomies.

Harmony was a harbinger of truth. It allows us to fit in with others while at the same time being as different as may be, because the idea of the whole is so grand that it can include all. Harmony allows *us* to be grand. This is what the idea of goodness was reaching for. But truth is infinitely grander: it meets all the demands placed upon goodness and then goes further by allowing us to dispense with the 'I' and with attempts to calibrate our relation to being and to each other. The unparalleled position of truth is revealed. Only now can we take a closer look at the ways in which human beings block its emergence.

CONCLUSION TO SECTION ONE

We have had to revise Plato's ideas in order for being and truth to emerge as unblemished absolutes. Only now can we adopt the Greek method of chipping away at all that keep these absolutes out of human reach. Primarily we must chip away at the social injunctions the mind uses as it attempts to substantiate the notion of self. Once free of them, the mind is a conduit for unlimited movement of thought. It allows conceptualisation to carry thought to the absolute. Here divisions melt away and truth waits to remove any residual obstacles. Instead of turning mind into an internal critic or taskmaster we can unleash the power of thought onto being. Philosophical method allows us to do this. Now all things begin to move. Thought takes an hypothesis or flight of imagination, and an encounter with empirical materiality, and then projects the thinker on a journey beyond the limits of classificatory thinking (laws, mores, conventions) that are said to limit what an individual can do. When the faculty of thought is allowed to engage with the ruminations of the imagination a veritable nuclear explosion takes place. We realise we can think about anything; we can engage with the as-yet-unthought. Philosophy shuffles the cards, plays with physical reality, with imagination, offers a 360 degrees vista, a depth of insight and congruent incongruities that leave the mind in a whirl, afloat on a cornucopia of intuitive possibilities.

Philosophy grants potency to critique beyond that offered by functional communication networks. It does so, not by opposing or accepting what the other presents, but by elevating the other beyond where they would otherwise allow themselves to go.

Thought and communication release untold aspects of the other and, as part of a feedback loop, of oneself too. Each riposte in a conversation builds on the last remark with glances back at earlier parts of the exchange, in a movement that engenders more than any one instance of the conversation will reveal. Untold facets of each person and of the relationship appear; swathes of not-yet-created reality take form and, eliding and weaving, they cut free from strict logic or reason. Philosophy is thus a method geared to the release of bounteousness.

And yet resistance to truth seems to arise in every encounter. I've pointed to the self as a portmanteau notion that covers a formidable array of obstacles to truth. Iris Murdoch sums up our daily task as '...the disciplined overcoming of self.' (1) In the next Section I assess the price we pay when we slip to the default position of the self.

SECTION TWO: REJOINING THE WORLD: FROM DICHOTOMIES TO CONNECTION

CHAPTER FOUR: THE SELF

'It was not only the man Socrates, but philosophy itself that turned, in his person, from the outer to the inner world.' FM Cornford, *Before and After Socrates.*

It is ironic that the notion which people desperately seek to substantiate - the self - is what stops them being themselves. Self emerges only when an entity encounters the world and then feels swamped by the encounter. The reaction, not the entity, is the self. It is half-born, an empty space filled by an excitation generated by an inability to explain a powerful engagement with being. It is an absence tantalised by animation. Indeed, the self and its twin, society, are intellectual conundrums. We can acknowledge the ontological status of the concept of being (in its new incarnation as the socio). And yet its products, the self and society, cannot claim this status. The socio colonised what is otherwise a simple idea of the self as a mere mark of identity. Yet this notion applies only to a temporary arresting of perception of the flux of being. And indeed an even more challenging realisation is that the person who arrests perception is also but a temporary arresting of perception. Perceived and perceiver are attempts to arrest or contain flux. Moreover, as Freud tells us, the idea of a perceiver is an attempt to control internal flux. Internal and external flux interact; the self that masquerades as a singular, substantial being abounds with the thoughts and feelings of others. The self then claims them as its own. All that is in us is prompted from outside; we are a hologram.

Self is a pre-philosophical notion which the inscription to 'know thyself' tells us is unknown. If we leave aside the individual body as the organism that 'experiences' the world the self is revealed as an organising and defensive move by the mind to impose order on a world perceived as inchoate. Even in pre-philosophical times it sat uneasily alongside the idea of the thing-in-itself, which held that the definition of all things lies in themselves alone. However the self can only be defined in terms of other things or otherness; it is unable to be its own subject of contemplation. Nonetheless it is a notion to which mythos allocated the function of observer of all things that can be defined. But the rise of logos moved the fulcrum of observation from the self to reality. Instead of the universe being in us, we are now a part of the universe.

Self was originally the characteristics of an individual, something that moves by itself; and soul was an individual's conscience. The breathing spirit or inspiration of the soul was the psyche. But psyche is now associated with the mind. Mind is the faculty that penetrates into meaning. The modern self is a re-conceptualisation of both soul and mind. The problem with the self is not its existence, whether as a subject of experience or as a notion, but its fixity. Were it to be conceptualised it might become more fluid and eventually find its place within the harmony of things.

It is not ontological or a thing-in-itself but a move to contain drives such as desire and revenge. In Freud's language the self is the ego and not the id. It is a calibrating mechanism that seeks a balance between society's call for rectitude (superego) and that which is natural or visceral in us (id). Yet the ego is only a notion devised to contain the superego - and the superego is society calling us away from truth! There is no need for the ego and by extension the self.

A person reveals merely the echo of the outside world when they explore an 'inner life.' The only time they connect with the totality of that outside world is when they wholeheartedly reach outwards to it. This move reveals the echo of the world that is a self for what it really is. The injunction 'Know thyself' fails, whereas 'know the world' allows us to *become known* as a second move. We must remember that the socio arises from human gregariousness. This pulls people together and then provokes a near-concomitant pulling away again as intimacy looms. The self emerges as part of this 'fight or flight' dynamic and is expressed in a pull-push form of relating. What is merely being's abundance bursting forth is construed as raw and threatening. In order to cushion people against these extreme movements the socio cordons off a middle ground where intimacy is not found, but neither is outright loneliness. Yet the absence of true contact leaves people feeling disaffected. Whereas philosophy accepts the world's terms; the self demands its own terms be accepted by the world. When the world will not conform - love is lacking or survival threatened - the human entity turns inwards and 'relates' to itself.

It is in this space that society arises in an attempt to regulate relations between myriad selves. Each self replicates internally the pull-push dynamic found between entities. The self is a micro-socio striving to reconcile its inner parts. Until it does this it is not capable of resolving its external relations. So, society is an aggregation of micro-socios involved in a variety of push-pull movements, possessing different histories and experiences, and standing on different rungs of the ladder of individuation. Despite these complexities, each of us is expected in the name of society to take responsibility for our many facets: we must contain some, deny others and burnish yet others. Society vaunts responsibility by imposing uniformity via legal-social norms. We are expected to reveal only those aspects of our complexity that gain general favour. We must not make public the fluidity with which the different parts relate.

Society has not yet emerged fully into reality. If we granted it ontological status we would be able to conceptualise it. If for a moment we anthropomorphise it we can say that it feels unloved, unsustained, that it has not yet been drawn into a conversation with the micro-socios that constitute it. It seeks a (philosophical) friendship in which major issues can be addressed. We enter sensitive territory here, but I'm thinking of issues like the relation of family to society that have long been left in abeyance. Socrates famously valued his time with strangers in the Agora above that with his wife Xanthippe. This is a philosophical point, not a personal one. Trenchant arguments raged over great topics In the Agora; in the family by comparison discussion was rule-bound.

To return to the self: it is faced with impossible demands. Society struggles with multiplicity (Heraclitus) and wants to impose one-ness (Parmenides). It denies the flux at the core of its member's selves because it has already abandoned its own core. It claims to be being but fails to raise itself above the bifurcating mind. So, at the core of humanity (and society) is a failure of human beings to be themselves. Ironically we are the opposite of what Plato claimed: at our core is flux while our appearance is uniform. In the *Republic* and *Laws* Plato appears to have begun to recognise, late in life, the dilemma that multiplicity throws up. He began to let go of a preoccupation with mind and to move to something grander. But it was too late. The key philosophical concepts to this day possess strong traces of self: mind, will, life, and the event.

We must cast our thoughts back over the self's history to see how this came about. In the time of mythos it was a term used to describe a person's identity and characteristics. However, humankind was then little developed. Mythos was characterised by adherence to habit, inertia and pre-digested views involving rituals and customs. Francis Cornford describes that time as devoid of leisure for disinterested speculation. Even in Homer there are no 'knowers,' only 'livers.' Homer describes his heroes by reference to animal names and behaviour. Each has a singular characteristic: Odysseus was cunning, for example.

Then, before the Pre-Socratic thinkers had more than a brief chance to direct their gaze out to the universe, its origin, nature and so on, philosophy in the guise of Socrates, started to direct its gaze inwards to the human soul. Irony of ironies, this move served to obscure truth. Mind was indentured on behalf of the individual soul. Philosophy became inward-looking. People took the universe into their minds; in effect they swallowed it whole. Meaning, momentum, wisdom and all matters universal begin to reside in the mind. Everything is as it is only because the self experiences it that way. This move had two consequences. Firstly, each self became a work of art, something uniquely special. What else is left when the universe is inside a being? Everything becomes a matter of decoration, elaboration. Secondly, the colonisation of the universe was an act of hubris, a pact with the devil that called for redemption. The price exacted was for each person to grapple with a tension that arose when they contemplated the difference between the ontological universe and its representation. The handling of this tension demanded some knowledge of the process. Herein lies the birth of psychology. By applying to myself what I would otherwise apply to the universe I can claim knowledge of myself. The drawback is that I can only know more about myself at the price of not being known by others. I turn inwards and hold onto a secret. Truth lies deeply embedded in my self - and it resists revelation.

The irony is that philosophy was complicit in this 'internalisation' of the universe. Once Plato mistakenly placed conceptualisation somewhere 'out there' in the universe the functioning of logos, of our ability to make sense of an intelligible world, was impaired. Having internalised the universe, humankind was now loathe to divest itself of it. Too much that was deemed to be human - heroism, excitation, excess animation, and erotic fantasy - would be lost. Philosophy promises to liberate truth - but life will then be less exciting; I will feel less special. I will become a mere part of the universe.

The self is now the last frontier for philosophy, the last bastion of an archaic version of truth, the last vestige of mythos carried over into logos. The universe has revealed its secrets to the mind but in the process we selves have become guardians of its form. A fascination with what we take to reside in ourselves has thwarted the search for universal truth. We no longer embrace totality. Rather, we are our own worst enemy. We only want truth to emerge from and to reflect human concerns, to fortify a personal aesthetic founded on nostalgia and trauma. My point is that *we* are truth if we subscribe to the notion of self. This is why the gist of this book is that the self is the enemy of universal, primordial and ontological truth. Self is a prison warder blocking truth's return to the world.

We owe this problem to Plato's struggle to understand the forces that move the world. His investigations took him to the gap between mind and being where self is born, and where we must go next.

CHAPTER FIVE: THE GAP BETWEEN MIND AND BEING

'Is [the decisive matter for thinking] consciousness and its objectivity or is it the Being of beings...?' Martin Heidegger, *Basic Writings*.

We have seen how the notion of self arose as an attempt to pin down flux or indeterminacy. It is a response to the quandary we face as we look out on the world and perceive a gap between us and it. As the mind thinks about incoming reality it notices itself thinking. Should it choose to go with the first thought or with whatever notices this thought? It cannot choose and instead panics and creates dichotomies, a gap. If we choose to rationalise this gap the observer and the observed will ossify into separate entities. Socrates' approach was to question the mind that perceives a gap and denies the wholeness of being. When we follow this move other possibilities arise. Classical thinking extricated us from dichotomies such as truth and non-truth by reconceiving the relationship: now instead it is between truth and the shadow of truth. A dichotomy reveals itself as a cover for innumerable possibilities. But we live in a shadow land still, and will continue to do so until we upgrade our questions about the gap between mind and being and treat the appearances it creates with scepticism.

Philosophy arises as we respond to the opportunity presented by the appearance of this gap. It must be emphasised that this is not a problem to be solved: it is an opportunity to live life to the full. Problems arise when we overinvest in the mind and so become embroiled in the view of the observer, or we over-privilege being and place everything in the other person. Heidegger claimed the

Pre-Socratics discovered a point of balance between mind and being. Nietzsche counteracted the tendency in philosophy towards mind by pointing to the earthy, visceral and wilful Dionysus. Their scepticism is well founded, for mind is unreliable. It emerges as an attempt to guard against the unpredictable flow of thought. This move generates logic, meaning and ethics. Mind soon becomes shackled by its own structures and in no time thinking has to accommodate to them. By then mind has forgotten that it emerged from thinking.

The Greek fascination with mind has led us astray. Mind is only one concept among many in philosophy. Thinking is the drive. Being on the other hand is more abstract and universal; it doesn't need to adapt to 'other' standards, such as intelligibility. A balanced relationship between mind and being might appear to be the answer. In ordinary parlance a 'relationship' indicates where an 'answer' lies. But being is fully itself; the 'it' here is a human category. Everything is in being. So why should 'it' relate to us? To be real is an oxymoron. We *are* anyway. Such a statement is equivalent to saying that being is a human being.

Classical philosophy warns us to be deeply sceptical of appearances. It asks how much of the whole lies hidden behind appearance. We must ask of every impression: is this a product of the mind? The mind observes itself observing reality and is confused. As a result it fragments reality and dichotomises wholeness. Heraclitus responded to this move by concluding that opposites attract. Gilbert Murray tells us that it was widely recognised in Hellenistic culture that every thinker had to 'listen to the other side' if truth was to be reached. (1)

The two grand hypotheses of mind and being are often seen as immovable bookends of a gap that is difficult or even impossible to bridge. But we have to go deeper into what this gap means. Firstly, mind and thinking do not amount to the same thing. The word mind is used loosely in common parlance. I use it to mean the notional space in which we can watch thoughts pass. Thought on the other hand is a force or reflective capacity within reality. It enters and leaves the human mind-space depending on the generation and reception of thought in the surrounding environment. Its entry to and egress from this space can be thwarted by the tight principles, unbending opinions and 'here I stand' nostrums on which we rely to bolster our sense of self and our place in life. Only in philosophy, as RG Collingwood put it, 'thought moves with perfect freedom, bound by no limitations except those which it imposes upon itself for the duration of a single argument.' (2) Mind is only a notional space possessing a propensity to become congested. It can appear to overflow onto being in an attempt to bridge the gap. This overflow is an attempt to control being; mind reacts as if being is the cause of destabilisation within the gap. However, free-flowing thought can bridge the gap. When thought is allowed to move unimpeded within an *open* mind-space it can respond subtly, creatively and expansively to the stimulus of being. In this way it allows the mind-being spectrum to adjust subtly.

Plato placed truth virtually alongside being because he disagreed with Homer's putting it alongside mind. Aristotle put it in nature or God. A human propensity to counter an earlier move is evident at the outset of philosophy. But Plato recognised something enduring - the seductive power that mind exerts over human beings. By associating truth with being he had already opened up three possibilities. Firstly, the idea of mind can be taken to a point where I presume he *intended* it to go, that is to say, to make being the supreme object of philosophical enquiry. This comment would be a truism had mind not dominated public consciousness for so long. Secondly, the Greeks reversed the usual direction of perception. Now, the world looks at us rather than us at it. A mind-oriented view would have us looking at the world as if we are outside it. Now we are part of wholeness, a wholeness that relates to us as an integral part. Thirdly, further revision of accepted thinking involves us in a long-overdue rereading of the three chief components of Plato's notion of harmony - goodness, beauty and truth. Truth can no longer be deemed secondary to goodness. Truth is nothing less than pivotal in the harmonising of being.

So the search for being takes us first to mind. But it must be emphasised that the problems we encounter do not lie *in* the mind; this is analytic and post-structuralist thinking. The mind *creates* all that we believe we are thinking. It is this 'all' that we take to be our problems. Classical thinking questions the mind; it doesn't judge or personalise it. Indeed, we can see that the mind is only an aspect of something much greater. Provoked by its classical antecedents, philosophy leaves the mind and its product, the self, behind and goes beyond both, beyond the way 'I know things,' to an area of knowing outside the reach of structured thinking. From this point onwards the way things appear to be becomes of secondary importance. The Greeks did something astonishing - by making the universe the subject and humankind the object they placed the fulcrum of everything 'out there,' thereby letting go of the self. Yet ever since there has been a recurring slippage in philosophy to second order issues. When things fail we let go of process and turn to content. When that fails we turn to structure or form. Plato slipped down this slope at the outset when he failed to treat truth as totality. The slippage continued - Nietzsche turned to aesthetics in reaction against metaphysics.

Socrates told us that there is a disposition in human beings to regress to what he called ignorance. The power of self, mind and social pressure takes over when we stifle movement in our thought. We do this most conspicuously when we confine thinking within conventions, within ordered or defensive attitudes or principles, or our own or society's narratives. People are never bad or deliberately stupid; they are borne down with anxiety about relationships, responsibilities and about the wellbeing of themselves and those dear to them. They may never have been encouraged to loosen the structure of their thinking or to question the workings of their minds. Indeed, unless we enter the furnace of philosophical discourse we will blame ourselves for what is rightly society's responsibility. All our rigidities start from outside ourselves and in society. In other words, without mental scrutiny and stimulation, our thoughts will sink into narcissism and selfhood and come under the hammer of the superego. This matters, because we recognise moments of truth only with an open mind. In those moments of openness being becomes real to us and we are reintegrated into the universe.

But we can go further - truth amounts to something more than an occasional access of being. As I realise something the something realises it too. In other words, our challenge is to let go of mind-constraints altogether and to connect directly with the other, with being. Mind cannot make a direct connection. Philosophically, all that has happened is that mind appears to have blocked up the space through which being can enter. Direct connection between mind and being is not possible. Franz Rosenzweig points out that something else has to happen:

'{The] immediacy of lived experience leads us as little as that first immediacy of cognition led us into an immediate relationship with the All. Cognition certainly had everything, but as elements, only in its pieces. Lived experience was beyond this bungled work; it was whole within every moment; but because always within the moment, it was therefore certainly whole, but within none of its moments did it have everything. The All, which would be both everything and whole, can neither be known honestly nor experienced clearly; only the dishonest cognition of idealism, only the obscure experience of the mystic can make itself believe it has grasped it. The All must be grasped beyond cognition and experience, if it is to be immediately grasped.' (3)

So, on the one hand mind cannot access being on its own; on the other hand being in its wholeness is not prepared to come over to mind. Why after all should the whole chase an errant part? Something extra is required to bring these disparate forces together: a lightning rod or catalyst. This is truth. In moments of truth all the dots are joined up, turning daily experience and abstract thought into two sides of the same coin. We can only presently speculate that more might be possible, that in those moments truth expands being and increases our mental capacity to reflect upon it. Both sides of the divide begin to appreciate the other more. This is profound enough. Yet truth keeps generating more and more potential. The magnificence of life is revealed when truth interacts with mind and reality to generate unlimited potentiality and thereby tests the limits of what it means to be a human being.

But this is speculation. All we can presently say is that we sink below the level of wholeness when we seek to corroborate things in order to be sure that a bit of being actually exists. We shun truth. We have entered the realm of selves, particularities and egos, of theory, dogma and scripture. This is the bailiwick of the priest, the one who claims to know and offers us a reassuring belief system on which to hold. No, the truth that has been ignored for so long, with the honourable exception of Spinoza, is monism or unity. It enables us to become who we truly are. It transcends and transforms everything because it lies between the observer and the world *and reveals there is no difference* between them. Certainly the more one observes the more differences appear. But this is because mind has started to expand to fill most of the mind-reality gap. Left to itself mind will rationalise the gap and turn the observer and the observed into separate entities, and then calibrate all the intermediate points in an attempt to get relationship 'right.'

Philosophy has to move fast to overcome that which it started - the use of the mind. Once we start freeing up thinking again we can return to Plato's 'source,' to the primordial. Then we can reverse our direction of thought so that it is based in being, shifting it to ontology and away from epistemology. As an example we can take a young child to be reality in the same way Nietzsche took Dionysus to represent nature. The child is more philosophical or authentic than a socialised adult can ever be. Reality, in the form of the child, already 'knows' in a pre-cognitive way. The adult can easily drown in thinking. The adult is the child plus informed knowledge. But informed knowledge has the power to disabuse the adult of the profundity of his deeper knowledge. No one wants to give up on informed knowledge and be revealed merely as a flow within being. But as we strip away the overlay of knowledge we reveal our being. It beholds us to be humble in the presence of children because we are in the presence of reality.

It is too easy to claim that truth is the revelation of being in its full glory. This statement fits with all we presently know about truth as a universal or absolute, which is admittedly little. But we do well to remember that we are seekers after truth - we will never grasp it. Socrates' method of questioning did not aim to reach being; this would have put being in the realm of knowledge.

The mind-being gap is not a problem; it can be left alone. It does nonetheless offer an invitation to be filled with relationship, the space for a dance to commence between mind and being. All we need do is let process run free in this space and accept that we can handle it. There is no need to panic and stop the dance. Nietzsche and Heidegger looked at the gap as providing the possibility of an emergent inter-subjectivity. This is the move I will explore further because this in-between field is productive of untold possibilities.

On the one hand, being reveals itself to those who are willing to perceive. Just looking out for it won't do. This is why this book is an exploration rather than a compendium of knowledge. On the other hand, truth only appears when certain requirements are met. These requirements are difficult to meet because we so often blind ourselves by assuming we need a belief system to sustain us. Before the rise of philosophy, religion was ascendant, and it is clear that the priest still beckons. Unmoved by belief systems the truth-seeker explores the gap and becomes no more or less than fully him or herself.

The key move is to conceive of the whole. In so doing, we can incidentally solve the ancient 'one-and-many' puzzle by putting it in the context of a personal life. A person then becomes at one with himself and with all things in the universe. Additionally, he becomes free of Christian sin, Sartrean bad faith and Freudian death wish. As he gains more confidence and steps further into uncharted territory other shibboleths begin to topple. For example, the early Greek hypothesis that truth connects us directly to reality took shape within a trinity that included goodness and beauty; this trinity characterised the harmony of the world. Yet, this idea of harmony is not inherently stable. If we put truth above goodness and beauty for example the idea immediately shatters. Greek harmony reveals itself as little more than an exercise in cultural symmetry.

So, when we give attention to truth we become involved in a major demolition job. Philosophy presently focuses only on the connections to being *that humans are deemed capable of making*. Philosophy has dealt with truth only as something which changes as its circumstances change. Universal truth is a step too far. To engage fully in this search, nothing less will do than to search for truth that connects us to being *in toto*. This is truth that lies beyond human authority; it is primordial, whole and a priori. Anything less is a product of mind and an example of being fracturing under the human gaze.

We have many threads to unravel. But we start with clear propositions. Truth is not knowable and thus not to be reached by epistemology. Heidegger goes further: 'truth does not exist in itself beforehand, somewhere among the stars, only subsequently to descend elsewhere among beings. This is impossible for the reason alone that it is after all only the openness of beings that first affords the possibility of a somewhere and of sites filled by present beings.' (4) He points us in the direction of something 'thingly,' ontological, primordial and pre-thinking. 'Before' beings there is a space. Beings can be beings only if they connect with this space. There, beings connect with others and with themselves. So, truth presents itself in the human realm (humans can search for it) while also pertaining to the world. But the human realm offers distractions and a reward system that obscures the world. The next three chapters explore the compulsive hold of self in human relations.

CHAPTER SIX: NARRATIVE

'The determined form I'm frightened of is certainly not anybody else's form [...]. [I]t has to do with being dominated by my own mythology, which is very strong.' Iris Murdoch, *The Philosopher's Pupil.*

The last chapter showed how, when the mind overflows into the mind-being gap and creates a rigid sense of self, humankind cuts adrift from being. Now we can look more closely at the way this tendency manifests in our daily lives: the creation of a narrative (or story, myth or text). Narrative re-enforces a sense of self. It is a role or part in a story we adopt in order to avoid social disapproval. Through the medium of narrative the virtually insurmountable force of society says: 'If you want to join the game, choose a role or job and run with it as far as you can go. Otherwise we'll not accept you.' We treat society as if it is reality and then adapt to its demands. And yet society is merely an accommodation of all machinations of mind in support of the notion of self, and the previous two chapters have indicated how unreliable this is. Our 'front' to being is something the mind constructs to protect it against its own apprehension when encountering being; this is a 'self.' Freud said a self manifests in the baby's reaction to its mother's gaze; Julia Kristeva sees it as a way of denying our mortality: the undeniable commonality of human beings. The mind might seek to show we are each different; the decaying body reminds us otherwise. Yet Freud and Kristeva treat a narrative as arising from the two extremes of life: early years and death. They deal with what we take a *human being* to be. Here I treat narrative, not as a human issue, but in terms of the universe - as an avoidance of truth. That is to say, it is a failure to face being, or to live a life of wholeness without remorse. Narrative is the denial of what Plato calls our divinity. For narrative is an idea disconnected from its source; it is more disconnected than a lie, which is merely the negation of its source.

Yet narrative's initial impetus takes it in the same direction as metaphysics. Both are ways of observing the world. They agree the world is harmonious and total; and that we are part of it even as we conceive of it. But then they diverge. Narrative protects the observer, the 'I' or self, the epistemological view of the world. But metaphysics doesn't need the observer or an 'I.' Rather, the metaphysician uses the ladder of mind to climb to a universal vantage point and then kicks away the ladder that supports the observer. The object is to capture something beyond the words, for philosophy uses language to upgrade words to concepts. The metaphysician so to speak takes the words of the world and inseminates them with ideas. Thus to argue for one narrative over another is to miss the point; the universal viewpoint of metaphysics is concerned with narration itself. To live outside a narrative requires that we take metaphysics' Olympian stand. In daily life it amounts merely to a humble recognition of the clutter in one's mind. A wry smile as I notice that I use my job to define my place in life is enough to modify narrative's aversion to reality.

Plato was fully aware of the powers of bewitchment arrayed against philosophy: 'The great Homer whom [Socrates} admits he has always loved, and the tragic poets must be banished from the ideal state, for they are but imitators of the life of visible nature and so paint an inferior view of truth. They "feed and water" the emotions and passions of men instead of restraining them by reason.' (1) In the end, he was saying, imagination and metaphor are given an impossible remit. They can only *claim* to connect us to reality without actually going there. They inflame the mind in acts of sorcery and mimic a move outwards to the world. Sitting firmly in mind's camp, narrative is unable to explore classical thinking's contention that truth emerges from the *interaction* between mind and being.

To understand narrative more fully we must place it in the context of previous chapters – as an aspect of the mind-being relationship. Behind narrative is the play of mind. Narrative extends mind's reach by inserting itself into the mind-being gap. It offers itself as a buffer between people and the world. This move seeks to impose a human stamp or authority, an anthropomorphic identity, on the indeterminacy of being. It does this by ascribing causes, values and content to being, thereby turning it into a plot-bound spectacle. The problem is that every time this happens it adds to an echo in the chamber of mind and leaves less room for being. At the head of this chapter Iris Murdoch points to the power of a personal narrative. By offering to swaddle a (socially-defined) vulnerable being from adversity it stifles movement of thought. Subtleties of difference harden into potentially antagonistic divisions. An inner life is the setting for mind-created demons to contend with each other for attention and the social arena becomes the setting for battles between self-fixated individuals.

Narrative's detachment from its source offers confirmation to two postmodern claims. Firstly, that the universe is inherently fractured (as by extension is philosophy) and secondly that we can only relate to the universe through language. In other words, the stretch and play of conceptualising, philosophy's modus operandi, is confined by language's structures. One narrative disappears to be succeeded by another; small narratives occlude into grand ones. Thus everything is text or narrative; there is no escape from words. Existence trumps being and self the world. A signifier doesn't need a signified. We can of course constantly reread the texts, a process that is said to release energy from within the container of form. Admittedly those who read a lot enter a greater reality than their personal narrative confers. They can traverse the text and come out on the other side into a greater sense of text. What is being revealed however is mind's aversion to being.

This aversion is in part a problem of language. According to Wittgenstein language operates under laws of Newtonian mechanics that capture a world through a series of nets. These nets always bring description to a unified form. Iris Murdoch wondered if description might sometimes slip under the net. But even then the early Greeks took description to be a second-order issue, offering a view of reality as a substitute for a direct encounter with reality. Roberto Calasso must have had this in mind when he said that language banishes the gods and turns humankind's gaze inward. (2)

But philosophy changes all this. It carries on when narrative falters. Certainly conceptualisation cannot occur without an alphabet that permits speech to form sentences. In fact the word 'logos' derives from a verb meaning 'to lay things side by side' or to arrange things in order to make a judgement of them. A developed alphabet appeared in Greece before Homer. The speech or logos of travelling reciters of stories was the background against which conceptualisation emerged. Logos, defined as the properties of a concept rather than merely as speech, appears only with Heraclitus. (3)

Before the emergence of philosophy a sequence of words was used to tell a story. The purpose of the story was to manufacture beauty. The order of words mattered more than the words themselves. Language was used in the service of form, itself regarded as sublime and beyond criticism. Philosophy turned all this on its head. Villagers who listened to travelling storytellers realised at some point that behind all the seemingly different stories lay a meta-story or story of stories – the idea of a story. Here is the beginning of philosophy or conceptualisation. Each and every word now potentially became a form. Words began to convey a meaning in and of themselves. They were now seen as a product of thought that is capable of being rendered to further thought. (4) The sequence of words now formed an order that obeys the logic of thinking. The purpose of language was no longer to capture what is outside itself. Rather, it became more like a self-reflection, where a mere sentence turns into a reasoned statement within which the meaning of words unravels in untold multi-forms. Language in itself is not wanting. Narrative requires language but language is not confined by narrative. Language serves a narrative-free philosophy well.

My point is that philosophy does better what narrative claims to do well. Both seek to uncover the code hidden in form: the drives, motives and fates that govern the way people treat each other. (5) Of course the call of narrative as a spectacle can be irresistible: the tug of the heartstrings as emotions swell, the sense of replenishment when a purple patch echoes in the soul, the reinvigoration of the myth of self, family, community or nation, the awakening to the power of fate, happenstance, or fortune. The more one loses oneself in the story the more one's existential issues rise to a higher pitch. Yet behind all of these responses lies the play of mind. The deepest feelings, the most vivid memory or association and the most strikingly imaginative flight of fancy hide unacknowledged assumptions. Storytelling is the thinly veiled story of mind. So it seems that, even as logos emerges, mythos takes steps to stop it.

In compensation narrative offers us catharsis, a temporary release from the very emotions that are generated by the avoidance of reality. Catharsis is art's professed benefit (according to Aristotle): a release from anxiety. Yet the price we pay for it is high. An apparently uplifting narrative can subtly transform into an insidious one, and one more cleverly hidden from consciousness. Even more worrying is the fact that the imagination that brings about catharsis is blind to the way it serves other forces. Narrative doesn't possess the capacity to critique itself. It is porous to socially mediated feelings, animation and values. It might relieve the heart temporarily, but it simultaneously introduces undeclared ways of thinking into a mind that responses to the tugging of the heart strings. In other words, imagination and the emotions elide confusingly, with the result that it is unclear how far they deviate from reality's promptings. This goes some way to explain why Plato castigated Homer: he was aware something serious has been lost when poetry claims to approximate to being. Narrative engenders both attraction and fear, which Freud tells us tend to interact. And no one stands up to challenge this move.

From the perspective of a particular – a self – being can appear unruly. Thus, an urge to make reality predictable is understandable. Indeed, Aristotle's words regarding tragic structure apply generally: narrative is a sequence with a beginning, middle and end. This refers to one's personal narrative (or family, clan, town or nation) as well as to artistic creations. When we seek certainty in an indeterminate universe we become texts; we will defend our narratives of career, gender, locality, taste and preference to the last. Kant and Freud can be called on to support this thesis: they tell us that the universe and a personal mind are structured. Yet all our observations of the universe emerge from the mind itself, making our observations unreliable. If we want to reach beyond appearances, Plato tells us, we must conceptualise. This must apply to truth. So it can be said that postmodernism is almost right – there is (almost) only the text. But there is a chink through which we might glimpse something else.

For example, Derrida talked about the *disruptive* power of philosophy. If we only follow the content of a discussion we risk missing the process that underlies the words. This is what I take the Greeks to have been saying about truth. Its ability to disturb all fixities extends to all the accepted connections between words and objects. When discussions adhere to a prearranged theme it is very difficult not to end up with a doctrinal conclusion. The absence of process may be summarised as doctrine in: doctrine out. Yet, if thought is to roam the world and we are not to be content with repeating learned mantras, doctrinal fixity needs shaking up. I take this to be Plato's message. He was not another priest offering dicta and verities, but a releaser of thought. Philosophy is discursive; it can move unexpectedly like a wisp of mist. It rests easily in the land of dreams; it arises in the ineffable, responds to drink, to a Dionysian surge of energy, to an altered state of consciousness.

Take the case of a friend who tells you, 'I am depressed.' Instead of merely commiserating or judging (which risks epitomising the emotional response that narrative elicits), one can respond philosophically in two ways. Firstly, one can take the universal vantage point (of Plato) and say that your friend speaks for everyone. Even today's statistics will back you up! Secondly, one can look at depression as an idea (or narrative). Now things change unpredictably. Attention has switched from the object of observation (your friend) to the notion or term (the narrative) that is being applied. This notion can now be made to reveal the unstated assumptions on which it is based. The heavy load of feeling around the word will lift and reveal untold possibilities. Discussion can release your friend from a prison of feelings and widen the context in which his or her thinking and life takes place. The possibility can be entertained that meaning arises out of life itself and not out of a codification of behaviour into acceptable roles; that meaning arises when we open ourselves to otherness instead of imposing a story foretold as the contents of Pandora's Box spill out.

Storytelling is the thinly veiled story of mind. Being just is, but mind construes it as unreliable and sets out in the guise of the self to control it. Like philosophy it seeks to find that which is concealed, but its search only highlights the mind's complex workings. The suffering caused by unfulfilled aspirations, slights, unrequited love, guilt, recrimination and frustration is interspersed with bouts of vainglory - the paraphernalia of an animated life. Mind has no sense that these responses are owed to its own workings. In this sense it is blind. But even if these emotions can be said to characterise most people's lives it doesn't follow that this is what is meant by the concept of being. There is in narrative an assumption that the release of emotions is enough if it draws the self (or reader or audience) into hidden personal worlds and evokes in him or her empathy or the response of 'There but for the Grace of God...' Moreover narrative dwells on personal predicaments that are absorbing to the self, reader or audience precisely because they have been normalised by society. We do not see ourselves in a narrative so much as notice the way society wants us to see ourselves. And we are not encouraged to question either this depiction or the very idea of an inner life that it posits. What is missing is an examination of being that questions the extravagant attention given to excitation, emotions and moods, and especially to the supposed container of all this repressed turbulence, the self.

A narrative-enclosed life is characterised by five features. Firstly, it treats individual lives as barely endurable. Sartre famously summed up this view as: 'We suffer, and we suffer from not suffering enough.' One individual is pitted against another. The resulting pain is given near-ontological status. Narrative is forced to mediate, calibrate, nuance and filter reality in an attempt to make life palatable or endurable. The treatment of life as an aggregation of unanchored fragments means that reflective humankind must be portrayed as fallen from grace, to be punished for being reflective. Frederic Jameson says, '...something in the very form of the novel warns us obscurely that things will not turn out – indeed, it is the very nature of things that they can never turn out.' (6) The assumption that human existence has been snatched from the universe is swallowed whole. The underpinnings of narrative are dislocation, loss, and a need to create a purpose. Reflection is made to bear the burden of a culpability that demands redemption. Of course stories are not ontological: they are not subjected to the test of irreducibility. Yet, all that we can know tells us that being promises a clarity, translucence, subtlety and nuance of engagement; a level of animation that draws us to others; room to play and gambol, laugh and cry - at the very least as much as a belief in a suffering universe would construe. And it is even worse than this. It is the use of narration as a shield against reality that confounds our thinking, heightens suffering, and tells us we have reached the limit of endurance. We are taken into the arena that Nietzsche calls slave morality, a cushioning from being, many times removed. Yet how much trouble has been caused by seeking to alleviate the unbearable? Who decides the limit? One of Iris Murdoch's characters asks, 'Why should life be endurable?' Aren't we asking minor-key questions?

Secondly, in its tragic form, narrative's failure to apprehend wholeness brings death to centre stage. As we enter the light we sink further into the darkness. At best we can but cope. Alternately we can endure the brief life of a hero. Young men enter an unwelcoming world where they must don the role of hero and pit themselves against the odds. But heroism is easily manipulated - the men fighting outside the walls of Troy became the source of countless legends. Yet they merely lived out a narrative given by a society that wanted to prosecute its wars. Seekers after truth have always had to struggle against the emotive pull of the animation that fills out narratives, both personal and public. However, classical philosophy deems reality to be lived outside the self. There, no one needs to be redeemed because no one is fallen. Inner anguish dissolves. Freud spoke for mythos when he claimed nature (id) is dangerous. The philosopher might comment: no, expand it; primordially the id is nearer to truth than ego or superego, or by extension narrative.

Thirdly, particularity reigns unchallenged. 'There is no normal' as one of Karl Ove Knausgaard's characters says. A character in Iris Murdoch's *Under the Net* exclaims, 'All theorising is flight. We must be ruled by the situation itself and this is utterly particular. Indeed it is something to which we can never get close enough, however hard we try as it were to crawl under the net.' She is referring to Wittgenstein. He talks of language being sifted through different sized nets to ensure that words form an order. Because narrative expresses reality as it fragments under the gaze of mind it is no surprise that narrative cleaves to the viewpoint of the isolated, alienated human being. It is akin to psychology in its concern with character formation. Socrates took thinking from an attention to custom to the formation of character; narrative picked up from this point. But Plato sought to move it on - from character to truth. Plato's parable of the cave addresses this issue. Philosophy arises as we look into the sun's rays outside the cave. The sun is taken as the source of all things. The parable tells us that we can start to think at the level of the absolute. In contrast, narrative arises as we look, not at the sun, but at the things separately illuminated by the sun's rays. Appearances and details are subjected to appraisal by the mind.

Narrative thus seeks to copy and interpret a fractured world. Indeed, mythos can be defined as the absence of a sense of completeness or interconnection. By focusing on the smallest detail, literature takes us close to the minutiae of a life: a self, refinement of identity, the mind's ruminations, a relation to another self, incidents and events. Instead of the writer receiving the sun's rays he or she observes the surrounding scene from a subjective stance. Everything becomes human-centred and mind-processed. Language dances to this tune. Human-created symbols or signifiers assume a status of their own, far removed from the object that is signified. A process of infinite regress appears; it becomes impossible to know who is writing and who reading. All of these moves can be seen as the price we pay for turning away from the sun, from the source of all things, and instead focusing on the things that the sun's rays out. Detail offers meaning, solidarity and connection to isolated individuals; it compensates for the 'crime' of seeking perfection. Indeed narration offers itself as a form of redemption, according to Jameson. The itemising of every detail in daily life in Knausgaard's novels confers a redemptive power that elevates the insignificance of daily life. The use of utterly prosaic language, indeed the very fastidiousness of its detailed treatment, seeks to lift it above pointlessness.

Fourthly, male heroism is a vehicle for mind. The era of mythos depicts Greek male heroes as exalting action, assertion, agitation and animation. The archetypal hero, guilt-ridden and prone, Achilles-like, to outbursts of extreme animation, perceives the world aligned against him and pushes against the pricks. This situation produced the cult of the hero, even though the young man believes he has no choice in the matter. 'My thymos is active' is a common phrase used by warriors in the *Iliad*, with reference to that part of the soul concerned with one's prowess in the world.

The final outcome of narrative's detachment from source is an 'inner life' that promises to find the self's bearings amid the indeterminacy of being. This is a creation of the mind; it arises from a human wish to ascertain, understand and formulate being. It is an outcome of consciousness's dissatisfaction with the formlessness of being.

Perhaps the only effective challenge to the potency of selfhood is an encounter with otherness: an intimate, lover or confidante. What actually happens when someone enters the force field of a self is that we are offered the opportunity to return to formlessness, that is to say, to being. Being is not bolted together into an end-on, shaped or seamless continuum. We may of course try to turn it into a compact, solid or interlaced entity. In other words, we force things - in the form of love, relationship or connection - into a shape that we can tell ourselves we recognise. This becomes a narrative that offers a sense of purpose or meaning. Yet it traps us. We try to extricate ourselves by calibrating how close to come to others or how to respond to them. We do not need to love or relate, to over-care for the other. The less we do the better in fact, for the other can cope. And to over-love or worry about the other is to infantilise them. Things will turn out as they will. To fear someone will collapse is to underestimate them (and being). We are not accountable for what happened before we met them. All we can do is to observe how we over-love them and relax and trust them and trust being.

So, when all is said and done, narrative is the voice of society. Nietzsche said that the moment we think we depreciate life and introduce the bacillus of revenge into things. The same could be said of narrative. By succumbing to society's imperative to define ourselves we contribute to a process that functions by *imputing* meaning and purpose to all things. A narrative is in other words something that we can claim functions, works, or gets things done. We slip away from ourselves, from being, when this happens. But at a more profound level we have also betrayed metaphysics or absolute thinking. We daren't leave the cave and look directly into the sun. It is here that philosophy starkly diverges from narrative. It is not the aim but the method that distinguishes the two. Narration expands the capacity of the mind so that it merges with other minds rather than loosens mind's grip altogether. It turns away from being.

CHAPTER SEVEN: EXCESSIVE ANIMATION

'If life lacks magic it is because we choose to observe our acts and lose ourselves in consideration of their imagined form and meaning instead of being impelled by their force.' Antonin Artaud, *The Theatre and its Double*.

Excessive animation can delude us into believing we are fully in the world. Emotional turbulence catches the eye. And yet it fails to reveal the operation of the mind that has generated it. We are preoccupied with mind because we are constantly drawn to an energy-sapping, obsessive search for internal resolution. This search is productive of excessive animation. Accordingly we feel complete and in no need of truth.

A process starts when I 'look out' at being. I have a sense that I am here and it is out there. Being has provoked a complex uncomprehending reaction in me. Animation rushes to fill the gap. Simple observation will not suffice; I cannot sustain this position of non-active involvement. Having tried but failed sufficiently to understand what is before me and in trepidation about my ignorance and the failure of my monitoring faculties to protect me, I react in one of two ways. Firstly, I might turn wonder into a love of the objects before me. In this case I will have injected qualities and meanings into the objects and then become bedazzled by the allure I have put into them. I then go further and tell myself I must possess these objects. I experience a sense of lack and devote myself to the acquisition or control of them. Or secondly, I feel threatened as I start to think about being. I associate being - that which is out there beyond my control - with indifference, even antagonism. Animation in the form of fear and doubt arises in me.

Both the above reactions - love and fear - are what Freud meant by hysteria, an eruption of feelings beyond what can be contained or channelled. Heightened animation can tilt into joy or misery or another emotion at the tip of a hat. We seem to have to pin down excess; unstructured sensation is unbearable. Our emotions become defined by the slightest margin of movement. Today the notion of animation has given way to that of excess. Both reactions arise because I have failed to comprehend the world. I have infused the world with more than is there.

Life is animation (or reflection) and being, or reflection and body. However Heidegger tells us we have split them apart, causing the alienation from the world that is so widely observed. We can easily fall into a Marxian dichotomising between thought and praxis. Certainly drama is action. We usually act to counter another on the assumption that something bad will result from their actions or thoughts. In this regard culture is a form of tantalisation because it leaves us dangling, quick to take offence and to march to war when we refuse to see the being that lies behind dichotomies. Yet when we let go of self and focus wholly on the other it becomes clear that thought lies *in* action, just as martial arts act through the other.

We fail to realise that the very nature of being is disruptive and unpredictable. This disruption is not a reflection on or caused by us. Getting hurt by life (or being) occurs as a matter of course. But we misunderstand being when we convert hurt into tragic suffering. When we detach animation from being we force each to look on the other with suspicion. We act this out in life by becoming fearful of the other. When we bring animation and being together again fear disappears. We stop treating what the other says as a personal slight and see it as merely the disruptive nature of being at work. We can stop offering reasons why the other dislikes us; we return to a state of 'that it is' and avoid the epistemological concern with 'what it is.'

Deleuze tells us that energy becomes blocked inside an entity when its identity hardens. The energy can overflow onto surrounding territory. Furthermore, the opposite can occur - an overflow can make entities harden their identity to ensure they are not overpowered by the strength of the overflow. A penchant for happiness is a case in point. Fear of the meaninglessness of the world might drive me to defend myself against it. I say I am happy to cover up this fear. I'll dress up, claim this restaurant satisfies me more than that one, laugh with the crowd, do anything rather than face the world's indifference with equanimity. I'll join others who fear the world rather than abandon social conformity and risk aloneness. Michel Houellebecq says we insufficiently sublimate when society blocks our path. More to the present point is Freud's belief that we defend against life, not against death. Culture especially defends against expansiveness, emergence of energy, and the strong freely using the extra something with which nature has endowed them.

Excess is fear of being. Lying behind all excessive reactions is a failure to be at ease as one apprehends being. They reveal a failure to just gaze and wonder, to leave things untouched and leave reality unaffected by social order. This failure arises not only from a sense of inferiority, timidity or fear in the face of being, but also from a feeling that the world has given me powers that make me stand out of the ruck, that place me beyond my fellow beings, and that I must now get back in line and submit to the prevailing fearfulness. A quick response might be to say to myself: Fred Bloggs is good at that; I at this. But this doesn't go very deep. I'm left thinking: why can't I accept that the world made me to be who I am? In my agitation I might even insist, as a defensive measure, on seeking knowledge of the world as a way of containing its impact. This is the route of science: an attempt to pin things down. Nietzsche said it is also the route of the fearful. In contradistinction, philosophy suggests we go no further than the initial state of wonder, and let the world unfold in front of us in all its glory. All that is actually happening is that I have become fascinated by the way my mind interprets the world. Nothing is wrong with the world; it just is! So, let us move beyond Freud and stop being neurotic. What if I stop monitoring incoming messages from the world, or internal impulses? Now I am taking Socrates' message as my source - the mind is the problem, not the world or my place in it. We need only tune into a deeper kind of knowledge than that offered by appearance or social imperative. Clearing the mind helps me realise that the cosmos is not a threat or an unwelcoming place.

A preoccupation with animus locates the source of human authenticity and integrity in an 'inner life.' We have returned to the territory outlined in the previous chapter. Yet classical philosophy views inward-looking-ness as inauthentic and derivative because it reflects the values of the zeitgeist and creates an 'I' or 'me.' Given that postmodernism tells us that an imperious inner impulse has taken us over, an impulse that prevents us receiving the sun's rays, the claim that life needs fortifying with excitation is at least logical. But the view that life is already over-animated is never explored.

For example, excess in the form of over-loving is evident in all aspects of culture. The prevailing message is that we cannot get enough love, as the Beatles told us. But love will not resolve a parent's dilemma over the boredom of a child or a friend's quandary about the depression of an adult. And yet everyone tries, to excess. Every time a problem is identified (by governments and charities most obviously) the intervention to put it right (though it might hit the mark in part according to temporary criteria) can only contribute further to the general problem. An attenuated version of the problem gets pushed further down the road. Karl Marx missed the point of philosophy when he said it was about changing the world. In similar vein, President FD Roosevelt was advised to do something, anything, rather than nothing, to nip the Great Depression in the bud. But, wasn't Sophocles telling us to pause before rushing in with solutions? Oedipus and Creon paid the price for imposing answers on little-understood questions. It is to be doubted that we are ever fully enough in the know to act with any certainty. Moreover, human agency shows an awesome disregard for the recovery powers of reality and a narcissistic reverence for the human ability to understand or anticipate reality. It also suggests a twitchy attitude towards personal responsibility, implying that someone possesses heroic qualities of nous ready to be applied to problems. But let us go further. What if a problem is not a problem? Could it be that the behaviour we identify as remiss and deserving of 'correction' is only so because our (over)socialised background points us in that direction? If we have not yet cleared suppositions from our mind a la Socrates, who are we to impose an action on complex, unfolding situations? What is the origin of this loving care? Is blind arrogance a cover for (understandable) bewilderment? Loving care is too easy and automatic a response when quiet contemplation or gaining others' views might point elsewhere.

Today's zeitgeist tells us to believe that human beings are only true to themselves when they are extremely animated. Animation is taken to be the human condition. This would be fine were the idea not misunderstood. When it is not exaggerated or contaminated, animation plays out a pre-culture, pre-language existence in which we are easily disturbed or rattled by the world *in the usual course of events*. Even this response can be seen as fine. But corruption creeps in. When we notice and think about our animation, things suddenly change. Animation is itself now seen as threatening. Thinking has distanced us from it; we then use our minds to build a narrative around our thinking about it. We attempt to interpret it, excuse it, judge it, forestall it, or make a drama out of it. We succumb to finding words to explain *what* is happening, what *appears* to be happening. People seem often to believe that reality is nothing else than the story we tell ourselves in an attempt to provide a cordon against the effect of our thinking about animation! All that has happened is that we were animated and we panicked. Nothing has actually happened ontologically; we've only thought about our animation and sought to signify it. Nonetheless, something further now seems to happen - mind starts to flirt with both animation and the narrative. By facing both ways, the mind seems to hedge its bets so to speak, presumably taking it that in this way it will not fall into the abyss. We have entered a shadow world where neither animation nor narrative can stand out clearly in its own right. If we take this to be the general condition of people, the task becomes one of bringing us back to simple animation.

The message of mythos is that life overflows with excess. Purgation was an ancient religious practice for removing excess humours. Aristotle called it catharsis; today we are more likely to call it excess. Indeed human excess is perhaps the chief problem faced by Homer's heroes. Roberto Calasso tells us that times were joyous and excessive when the gods descended from Olympus. In the *Iliad* 'My thymos is unstable' is a common remark referring to that part of the soul concerned with getting on in the world. Many heroes indulged excessively in loving or hankering after other people and things. The chief cause of excess was hubris or pride, the inability to know how far to go. Sisyphus falls into this category, as do Creon, Oedipus' uncle, and Laius and Jocasta, Oedipus' parents, who, having been told by the oracle that if they had a son he would kill Laius, went ahead. Antigone knew she might die if she defended her brother Polynices' right to a burial, but she persisted.

An excess of animation tells us there is a mismatch between intention and outcome. Thoughts are associated with given actions. (Stage One: I say that I know more than others. Stage Two: I then think my remark sounded arrogant and I must apologize. Stage Three: I believe my apology has demeaned me. Stage Four: I am angry about the imagined diminishment involved in the act of apologising. And so it goes on!) In Freudian terms, the ego has had to mediate between the unruly but authentic id and the over-critical superego. A tiring and unstable life ensues in which I struggle to get on with people around me. Freud and his analytic followers tell us that this is all we can expect from life. But Freud built on an assumption in mythos that a newly arrived baby must fight for its given Moira or space in the world. This assumption takes it that merely being alive provokes resistance from others. The part of the psyche (or soul) known as the ego then adopts a monitoring role in the space between the admonitory mind-force that is the superego and the primordial id. However, this move obstructs the search for truth, which is associated with the id. So, instead of monitoring the effect of the mind on being or the primordial world, we can clear away the layers of social debris that smother the id - and then let the id speak to other ids, whether uncovered or not. This demands courage.

Indeed, to the extent that one lives a life of excitation and risk one must accept its corollary - that life becomes an exercise in problem solving. Relations with others will become complicated as layer upon layer of neurotic excitation builds. And all this happens despite the fact that we are never faced with ontological problems in life, only with ordinary ones. Extracting ourselves from our private mythos is not a major task when we realise this. Ontological problems take their course regardless of the thoughts and feelings we associate with them. And ordinary problems are amenable to ordinary solutions. Moreover, problems only arise when we consider ourselves to be an 'I.' Only when we free ourselves from containment by the 'I' can we ask what it means to be human, because we are not who we presently think we are! Of course we possess mind-determined futures and histories, but if we limit our freedom by allowing these thoughts to escape questioning we will stop being human in a much fuller sense.

This is not to bemoan frailty; it is to affirm the potential to go beyond hyper-animation. Then we can stop thinking about the thinker (who is human) and look at things from under the aspect of eternity. Otherwise thinking about oneself generates lines of defence that will sap our energy. They become self-defeating. Cognitive psychology can loosen a few lines of fixed thinking and rigid behaviour patterns. But it merely pushes the can further down the road, as far as freedom goes. We might greet the loss of all coordinates with fear. But we have most likely become fearful because our thinking is contradictory. We need only remind ourselves that contradictions arise from within consciousness and we immediately know we have slipped to the mind side of the mind-reality spectrum and lost touch with being. The remedy is once again to look outwards to others.

The only aspect of life that stays calm in the face of our panic around animation is philosophy. It invites us to retrace our steps to their origin, which is always outside the self, the only place where human beings are free. Philosophy takes us back to the moment preceding the construction of a self or narrative. Descartes tells us we fully know we *are*. Moreover, it is indisputable that we *feel*. Philosophy asks us something else: to face up to the feelings that arise *without trying to explain them*, without turning them into a construct. It is undeniable that we feel most of the time; what is to be disputed is what we say about it. Because what we say can drive us to intensify our feelings. We seem to know no other way to channel these feelings than into a narrative. But narratives are untruth. We can never know or describe ourselves.

The philosopher's task is to complete philosophy's birth process. The alternative is for philosophy forever to make concessions that deny its full potential. Free of excessive animation it can stand alone. Animation will no longer restrain the power of reflection. Rather, it will provide a jumping off point into further thought.

CHAPTER EIGHT: EROS

'...the fragile nature of the bridge that love throws between two solitudes.' Alain Badiou, *In Praise of Love.*

A search for truth becomes a journey from Eros to agape. Eros is the god of love. He represents a generalised self that seeks to control the flux of being. Love is a manifestation of truth only to the extent it seeks to unify separate fragments of being. But, once two people have become a couple the desire for self-pleasure it has instilled in the lover stops the couple moving on to agape (or being). The Greek word Eros translates as 'to conquer.' By breaching the boundaries of another's self it can lead to the fusing of two beings. Agape on the other hand describes a heart that is great enough to embrace all people without seeking to fuse with a given one. It is a state of being that engenders equable, accepting friendships. The journey from love to agape carries philosophy out of its childhood in mythos into the mature adulthood of logos. It is a move from possessiveness to fondness and from the rules that govern the domestic hearth to the rumbustious exchange and open intellectual air of the Agora.

Eros is the Greek god of energy and bewitchment that provides the impetus for lovemaking. He draws two people together. The *leaving* of Eros occurs when each partner realises how different and complex is the personality of the other to the point that in key ways the other challenges the very pillars of their self. Self fights back. Arguments ensue, defensive positions are taken up and the relationship is put to the sword. The only route out of disaster is to anchor the relationship in metaphysics, which requires one or both of them to commence a journey to agape.

What does this involve? We must turn back to Plato. He delves deep into this human drama. He is making the bold claim that an equalised love between two adults is impossible. He speaks for philosophy here: its first move is asymmetrical and unidirectional. It begins in the moment a person's fascination with the world or being drives them outside the self, the family and society towards another being. In other words love arises in one person; it has nothing to do with equality, symmetry or reciprocity; it does not demand requital. Rather, it has, as an initial step, to do with someone being touched profoundly by the hidden reality of another. Plato is reminding us that being is hidden by all that makes up a self - a cluttered mind, social convention or narrative. But his move forces us to think more deeply. Behind the attraction to the beauty of the other something else beckons. The lover perceives a denial of being, an acceptance of stasis, in the chosen one. The lover is able to make the initial move because they can handle the brickbats that life has thrown at them better than can the beloved. Whether or not consciously understood, the release of the being that is hidden in the other becomes the lover's goal. The lover is able to return to sad memories without being overwhelmed by them. But the beloved is stuck 'in the depths.' This is also Democritus' term for truth. The lover is in search of truth in the depths of the other. The beloved has developed a self hoping it will equip them to survive among other people who have adopted this way of facing old pains. We talk of 'falling' in love. The lover invites the beloved to return into the depths, but now accompanied by a lover who will not waver as the beloved takes faltering steps. The lover may open to more being but the move is on behalf of being itself. This is not a human-centred move. Love, like philosophy, is an invitation to enter the depths where being and truth lie hidden.

For Plato this asymmetry tells us something profound about being. Unconcealment, as Heidegger was to call this move, is the recognition of a force greater than oneself. It tells us we are in the universe; the universe is not in us. When we realise this we are free. But Plato saw how difficult was the successful completion of the process. For example, the lover's gaze can stop the process by transfixing the beloved. This act of incorporation would be a triumph of selfhood; two selves into one, so to speak, as hinted at in Badiou's remark at the head of this chapter. But Plato wanted to protect the integrity of being (in this case, the beloved or object) from the narcissistic demands of the lover or subject. Descartes' Cogito subsequently helped us think more deeply into the ways an 'I' might become embedded in the object. The more recent attempt to rescue the (female) object from the (male) subject can be seen as in a sense a reaction to the Cogito. However, Plato's profundity took him beyond aspects of human relating and onwards to truth. He is making two points. One: the lover seeks truth by way of the beloved. He or she might delight in the beauty of the other but they are aware they are playing for higher stakes. Two: the higher stakes involve the lover in appreciating love as love, that is to say, in recognising that love is ontological. The love relationship is a human matter; the true or ontological object is love itself. And the way to understand love is to conceptualise it, in other words, to be philosophical.

The philosophical canon's treatment of the love relationship is now profoundly anti-Plato. It is profoundly pro-self. Plato's realisation that loving is unidirectional suffered disapprobation in the 20th century because its seeming inequality offended prevailing egalitarian sensibilities. It in effect says that love can only arise between a parent and a child. Love between equals, even mature adults, is impossible. Only friendship is up to this task. Maybe philosophy is harsh in its directness. But Plato is making a daunting philosophical move. He is saying that, in contradistinction to love, friendship is the only possible long term, adult-to-adult relationship. All else is hubris and doomed. Relationship can only begin when the integrity of the beloved is respected, and for that to happen the lover must be selfless. This is where metaphysics comes in. Plato conceived of a love relationship as one in which mind (the lover) reaches out to being (the beloved). Loving now seeks to reassert humanity's place in the universe. Yet, because we see ontology through epistemological spectacles, it is a challenge for a couple to appreciate the profundity of this journey. Plato's point is that, unless mind bends in that direction, a relationship will soon fail or become hollow. In other words, there are *only* philosophical relationships.

Despite Plato's challenge to romantic, erotic and self-centred love, later attempts have sought to retain the human element in love. Heidegger turned the two lovers into *objects* or recipients of the gaze of the universe; both were *receivers* of love. This was a strong gesture towards the Greek attempt to elevate love to metaphysics. But it was an awkward half-way house. Badiou considers love between two subjectivities to have created a larger *subjectivity*. Existentialism sought to express love as a utopian relationship between two thoroughly worked-through, well-intended *subjects*. Both gave of themselves equally, in step with the 20th century's drive towards equality. Sartre did however admit frankly that a relationship based on personal responsibility was impossible ('Hell is other people').

Because Eros brings about the convergence of two particularities, two separate minds, the danger of creating a folie a deux is ever-present. Indeed convergence might move from illusion to delusion. In both people presentation has detached itself from being such that presentation meets presentation.

So, to return to Plato: he underlined the Greek contention that love is ultimately a way of reaching beyond our ego-selves to the world. Initially love allows us to relate to the other with greater acceptance and understanding. More being enters. We are drawn into an appreciation both of the uniqueness and universality of the beauty of our beloved. We are reminded of the being we have lost. Yet the problem is that being is total while life appears to us as a multitude of perceptions. A lover carries an awareness, even if only that, of the reality that lies behind perception. Plato puts it thus in *Phaedrus*: 'And this is nothing more or less than a recollection of those things which in time past our soul beheld when it travelled in the company of the gods and, looking high over what we now call real, lifted up its head into the region of eternal essence.'

In the lover's eyes the beloved possesses something barely apparent to the general eye. Alain Badiou exhorts us to 'love what you will never see twice.' (1) He doesn't mean identity, which lies on a socially-defined spectrum. He means the other's disconcerting uniqueness. Lover and beloved feel deeply connected and threateningly separate at the same time.

This takes us back to Plato's conceit of the lover as mind reaching out to the beloved as being. Being is as it is: indifferent, even opaque and sufficient unto itself with regard to the lover's approaches. It is relatively immune to blandishments. Thus, the momentum of the encounter owes everything to the ardour of the lover. The lover is usually seen as a man, but this ignores the subliminal messages that pass between people. The issue is not crudely defined by gender. But, for the sake of this account, I will treat the lover as a man. Persistent wooing by the lover has created in his mind a beloved in his own image. He risks falling in love with what he has created, however little relation this creation might bear to the actual person of the beloved. He is likely to find fault with aspects of the actual person that do not fit this image. Equally he might be terrified he has become a Pygmalion who is falling in love with his own creation. Moreover, to return to the Greek theme that runs through this book, disillusionment with the beloved only refers to what is apparent, to what he *perceives* her to be. What he has failed to see must be taken into account if he is to relate to the whole person. Otherwise, in philosophical terms, he will lose contact with the whole and only connect with the part. I return to my philosophical conceit again - the beloved stands for an indifferent and relatively opaque reality. Mind is wooing reality. But this means that a part is wooing the whole. Why should the whole adjust to the part? The momentum and outcome of the relationship owe almost everything to the ardour of the lover (mind). Yet he is hampered by a lack of self-knowledge, that is to say, knowledge of how mind operates as it engages more closely with reality.

In the *Symposium* Aristophanes offers a context in which we can see the erotic phase of love working its way through. Humankind was guilty of rebellion in heaven, he says; as a punishment it was split into men and women and then ejected from heaven. Subsequently man has been looking for his other half in order to return to heaven. This story suggests that the other completes us.

But let's go further. The word erotic is a coming together. But what is togetherness? Socrates' muse Diotima explained how we know the other is truly our missing half. She wasn't concerned with cultural, educational or emotional issues, but about feeling we've met that person before. ('It's as if I've known you all my life,' as the saying goes.)

Plato expresses this in the *Symposium*: '...someone closely aware of the mysteries of love, sees in another face a reflection of heavenly beauty; terror and awe thrill through him at the remembrance [of what it was like in heaven] and if he didn't fear being castigated as mad, he would treat the beloved as a god.' If we stay with the idea of the other as the missing half it is easy to understand Diotima's claim that, when we fall in love, we are really falling in love with ourselves or the repressed parts of ourselves. We are seeking wholeness, completion, that which is missing. Desire is said to be lacking what it desires. This is because we think we have gaping emotional wounds. Yet by becoming reconciled to these wounds in the other we can begin the process of accepting our own dark or neglected side. The beloved represents our own injuries writ large. No wonder we are attracted: joining with the beloved offers us the prospect of completion of our individual selves. Yet we have not left selfhood.

Thus the early stages of a love relationship are concerned only with self-pleasing. A state of union is mimicked. Even when connection is not merely predatory, it at best seeks to repair a fractured being ('I need you, cannot live without you'). The dynamic of a love relationship reveals the early stages of love to be an unconscious act - when we talk of 'falling in love' we become a slave to feelings. It is an intoxicating, often overwhelming sensation that seems to put all things right and make one feel larger than life. We have fused with another and feel complete.

The intoxication of the state of infatuation is based on unstable factors. Spinoza tells us that we fervently hope the other will return our feelings while we dread they won't. We are leaving everything to the caprice of fortune. Certainly this state releases us from the attempts we usually make to impose order on our lives. This may be the only time we nakedly face life since being a baby, totally open to intimacy, unprotected by the defensive walls we erect later in order to avoid getting hurt. Here instead we are subject to forces beyond our understanding. Presumably this is why the Greek gods believed the god Eros was too unstable to join the Olympian assembly.

When mind starts to engage with being, the lover is forced to handle his own narcissism. He is forced to ask himself if he is searching for a person or for reality. Were he to face his beloved as both a channel to being and as a normal human being at one and the same time he would perceive the opportunity for them to dance with each other. A fresh breath of reality would then deepen the resonances of the relationship. To see her as an entry to being requires him to let her stand alone in her full glory. To do this he must face his own demons. This is her (and being's) gift to him. Only then can a fulfilling and lasting relationship occur. A relationship is not a battle between particularities, that is to say, between two minds. Neither is the beloved a particularity on which the lover can press his narcissistic demands. Were he to act in this way the push-pull energy that characterises over-loving or passionate encounters would overflow. The relationship is not between two people but almost wholly between each and being.

112

Mind has to cede to being. The lover has to face the reality of the beloved. The words of the beloved no longer provoke a negative response because they represent only the content of what passes between them. By placing the words in the widest possible context he can engender a process between the two that anchors the relationship in being.

Now the possibility of agape arises. Free of the play of mind, the lover rises above the romantic fog generated by Eros and looks to the long-term vibrancy of the relationship. The earlier bewitchment is now seen to be unreliable and shallow. Agape is a thing-in-itself. It is friendship free of symbiosis. It is logos in embryo. Responsibility for the relationship overrides that of each partner for the other. Doubtless, the beloved is little aware of the philosophical work being put in by the lover. She treats it with indifference, just as life or the world is indifferent to humankind. Rebuff follows rebuff; the beloved will never know what the lover is doing. The lover is tasked to stand by the beloved irrespective of her ignorance of what is happening, without sermonising, criticising or spelling out what is happening, or wanting praise for what he is doing. The effect of lasting relationship is to open a space between the partners for being to enter. This requires one of the couple to be cognisant of the needs of the other without seeking to rescue them from these needs or collapsing under their weight. Otherwise a relationship will quickly fail. Kierkegaard realised that 'the relationship is the absolute, not the accident of [meeting] a beautiful girl.' Now love becomes an invitation to anchor the relationship in metaphysics, that is, beyond the self.

Socrates offers us another model to that of erotic convergence. Like other Greeks who lived life outside the self he spent most of his time in the hurly-burly of life in the Agora. Here inter-subjectivity, not subjectivity, prevailed. This is agape in action. All issues in the community were discussed without fear or favour. Personal life - subjectivity - was left to the domestic sphere. Today this is changed; all is subjectivity within an expanded domestic sphere that attempts to capture the soul by fusing separate selves or subjectivities into one entity. This is clearly doomed; cohesion tightens ever more around the family. This social practice is supported by Freud's view that society is underpinned by the coming together of four subjectivities - father, mother, son and daughter. The diminishment of life into the tight bounds of a love circle that has never progressed to agape makes it shallow, constricted, a veritable soap opera. For it barely to maintain itself it needs bolstering by art, culture and the media. The potential for opening up deep and profound issues vanishes. The self and subjectivity have won a Pyrrhic victory.

But, for those who will go beyond self the possibility exists for active loving to take the maturing relationship to a third stage - from mature love of one to love of all, with its concomitant of a love of ideas. The poet Fernando Pessoa said 'love is a thought.' Now we no longer relate as one self to another self but as a human being to reality. Of course, self is a dogged adversary. Giving it up might seem to take us to a place of utter loneliness; this is where the call of self is strongest. But we can always remember that the self is only a notion. And when we relate to the world or to otherness, when the latter eclipses self, we've actually grown up at last. We've let go of the wish for others to heal our wounds. We can be friends - indeed some argue we cannot offer friendship until we have accepted this oceanic loneliness - and we can handle a degree of straight talking. Once we have faced outwards to the world we can turn to others with equanimity, but not before. Mythos tells us it can divert us from loneliness by telling us stories, by becoming highly animated, or by fighting the world heroically. But by looking from beyond ourselves we have crossed a watershed. We've gained the chance to see life in all its stark yet luminous reality. We have become a truth-seeker.

CONCLUSION TO SECTION TWO

A return to the world can get underway now that self has retreated. Thinking becomes oriented towards the world. Self-regard, introspection, particularising, dichotomising and taking up positions less and less hold us prisoner. Thought can be processed as or soon after it enters the mind and a response can be given to the world that resonates more closely with what has entered. What has not been understood can be explored by asking others how they 'read' the situation. Otherness need no longer be perceived as a threat to the ego but rather as the chief way to know what lies beyond selfhood. Rumbustious public discussion can chip away at residual elements of social training and keep open a channel to the world.

The blockages discussed in this Section pulled our thinking up short before we were able to contemplate transcendence. The transcendent can never be attained but it pulls us into the world. Without it nothing external to us is available to inspire or challenge us. Blockages imprison us at the human level of awareness, merely offering insights into a world 'revealed' to an inward-looking eye, which is the thinly disguised self as mind-at-work. There is no way of knowing how these insights relate to the world at large or how far they are an internalisation of the mores of society. They prevent an exploration of other, more profound, versions of being human. The problem is the mind. It doesn't know how to observe itself. The mind lacks knowledge of the other. It cannot locate the whole of it. It panics and overdoes the search, acting as if it is meeting another observer. It is rather like politicians who ignore the grand issues in order to assassinate their opponent's character.

A calm observer would leave the situation to unfold. Even a short delay allows more reality to emerge. Greater comprehension is possible the longer the delay. But society pushes us to act! Can we resist? Because, now that mind is less assertive and the point of balance on the mind- being spectrum has swung towards reality, new prospects beckon. Metaphysics comes to the fore. Transcendence raises our sights. Thinking can roam more freely, opening up untold possibilities.

All these blockages treat thinking as if it possesses an inner energy that has to be released before life's movement can occur. Yet the opposite view has much to commend it. Thinking (once released from the structures we call mind) is sufficient unto itself to 'move' life; life is all we need ask for. In other words, life does not need supercharging; it is enough that it moves at its own pace. To see thinking otherwise is to doubt its efficacy. To wish for more from life than it provides is narcissistic. Such a wish arises out agitation and dissatisfaction with a life lacking relaxation and equanimity. It suggests a life centred on a human point of view. I argue that things calm down when we *receive* reality and let it call all the shots. If life is supercharged by human will, aspiration, agency or love, we will end up with narrative rather than what lies behind narrative, excessive rather than ordinary or natural levels of animation and Eros rather than agape. Conceptualisation will fall into the hands of narcissism.

We are now free to move the fulcrum of thinking into the world. We can use the tool of conceptualisation. This is a pivotal shift in our search. It enables us to harmonise our thinking. We can think expansively without needing to resolve every logical contradiction. But conceptualisation cannot *make sense* of inflowing reality; it cannot bring about unity. Reality manifests in many forms. We are not yet able to make sense of the placement of these forms because they overlap, elide and play with each other. We are still getting to know what it means to know connectivity! Nonetheless, having bridged the dichotomies that broke the connection to totality we can now raise our gaze to the further peak of unity.

SECTION THREE: TRUTH EMERGES: FROM CONNECTION TO UNITY

122

CHAPTER NINE: CONCEPTUALISATION

'The concept is a whole because it totalizes its components, but it is a fragmentary whole. Only on this condition can it escape the mental chaos constantly threatening it, stalking it, trying to reabsorb it.' Gilles Deleuze and Felix Guattari, *What is Philosophy?*

Here is our first awakening to truth. It is the process of conceptualisation that carries human beings beyond human faculties. It is human freedom, the divine in humanity. When we conceptualise we leap from human mind-construction to an entirely different category of thought, A human being can create a concept and believe their mind has created it from scratch. And yet they have actually discovered something that is there already. They have partaken in a generative process they can only access. Creativity has opened a door to an eternal realm. In this realm signification is revealed as nothing but a human convenience. We can now suspend the idea both of an observer and an observed (mind and reality), for they are but ideas. Were we to preserve these devices we could even consider reversing them - life lives (or conceives of) us, as Derrida suggests. But perhaps still more startlingly, we can let go of reality. In Chapter Four I pointed to self as no more than a notion. A claim to reach out to reality is a human claim (self makes it). Yet the intelligibility of the universe is not dependent on human intelligence. It is there anyway. Deleuze talks of reality breaking up into many pieces. We get glimpses of it in the form of fate, science or happenstance, but the intelligibility of the universe may not be accessible to Newtonian or Einsteinian categories of thought. We cannot after all claim to access the universe in our own image. So, if our intelligence does not determine the issue, neither does the intelligibility of the universe. The universe will not help us in our search. So we must accept that there may forever be more in the universe than we can find. We can now see why the Greeks equated reflective thought with being. For the philosopher there is only the process of conceptualisation. Everything else is a simulacrum.

In any case primordial truth is a process or force that invites our *involvement*. It doesn't respond to attempts to stand outside and define it. We have now reached a point in our search where we can notice when the mind attempts to separate us from being. Mind presently lies in a resting, receptive state, unburdened by opinions, assertions and theorems. In other words conceptualisation takes us beyond the remit of experiences, appearances or structured thinking. In this way more aspects of reality can enter a conversation; thought can become elastic and porous to what has not yet been conceived by existing thoughts. In this state of intellectual fluidity and unassertiveness the play between mind and being becomes a dance, a mutually generative interaction. Truth can find a welcome in this space.

But as thinking opens up to totality we realise we are not out of the woods yet. The absolute promises so much and at the same time it throws up fresh problems. For example, it tells us that when we think to this level we are already *there*. Accordingly it closes down other 'theres' or other moves to infinity or inconclusiveness. Yet the incomparable advantage of the absolute is that it is able to recognise its own opposite. In this way it becomes Aristotle's excluded middle. Nietzsche saw the absolute as an airy idea, but Heidegger saw it as a connection to non-being. It connects to its shadow or echo and is thus pregnant, emergent.

Metaphysics resolves the problems thrown up by the Fall, that is to say, by the emergence of mind and language. It takes us 'back' to a place before mind and language introduced division into being, to a place where only difference obtains between things. It does this because it realises that mind and language are manufactured by the mind (yes, the idea of mind is produced by mind itself!); they are not intrinsic to being. At bottom it resolves issues that arise between the parts and the whole. The existence of parts does not threaten the integrity or rupture the seamlessness of the whole. Put in human terms, we can be fully ourselves without limitation or distortion, because reality is so grand that it can accommodate all differences. This enables our magnificence to be revealed in its full grandeur.

The role of harmony in mythos was to fit all the parts together into a whole. Logos now gives this task to truth. But, in logos, reflection is at risk of being trapped in mind. Were this to happen divisions would emerge between the parts. Something is needed to loosen up the tight grip of mind and allow the boundaries of the parts to be dissolved if beings are to move unhindered within being again. This helps to explain why absolute or metaphysical thinking is *the only* thinking. We are not faced with a choice. All other thinking seeks to divide being. Absolute thinking allows meta-concepts to arise as fixed positions collapse. At the absolute level all thoughts find their place within the whole. None is wrong. It becomes possible to accept one argument and its opposite at one and the same time. It is in the performance of this task that truth is capable of facilitating human freedom.

But the history of ideas moves on. The concept of the absolute has been corrupted. Once used to describe the kind of thinking I've outlined above, it has come to mean a rigid idea or an end-point. Like metaphysics, it has almost vanished under Nietzsche's assault on behalf of selfhood. Philosophy has suffered as a result. When Nietzsche proclaimed God's death all absolute claims were deemed null and void. And what I have indicated as absolute thinking was swept away too. Representation was cut adrift from ontology, existence from essence. Life now contends with limits; fate tempts desire with intimations of tragedy. A sense of wholeness is deemed unattainable, even laughable, because life and thought amount to no more than an exercise in picking up the pieces that an indifferent universe has scattered and in then trying to make some sense of them. It is as if life amounts to little more than a reaction against being's indifference. Aspects of mythos have returned with a vengeance. The traction for this approach comes from thinking that says that absolutes or totalities fail to take account of the one who thinks about the absolute. Thus the very kernel of post-structuralist thought is a dismissal of unbounded thinking.

Yet without this method we cannot journey to truth. For truth does not arise from the world (the many) or from the 'I' (the one) but rather from within the domain of Plato's return to the world. It has to be conceived of as a process; it cannot be reduced to a fixed position. The process involves opening up ideas, not the reverse. Dialogues between friends who accept each other's rough edges and can keep their eyes on the virgin territory that opens up once opinions are abandoned - these are dialogues that exemplify absolute thinking. Classical thought understood the dialectic to be a to and fro conversation in which the possibility existed that all positions might collapse. But as we approach the whole, that is to say, as our thinking becomes less and less structured and ordered, the process too often appears to falter. 'The problem of philosophy,' says Deleuze in *What is Philosophy?* 'is to acquire a consistency without losing the infinite into which thought plunges.' Tension arises when the prospect of facing into the sun becomes immanent. Nietzsche implored us to hold firm at this point, for 'Will to truth is a making firm, a making true and durable, an abolition of the false character of things, a reinterpretation of it into beings. "Truth" is therefore not something there, that might be found or discovered - but something that must be created and that gives a name to a process, or rather to a will to overcome that has it itself no end - introducing truth, as a *processus in infinitum,* an active determining - not a becoming-conscious of something that is in itself firm and determined.' (1) Yet neither Nietzsche nor Heidegger pursued truth to its source and Sartrean existentialism cleaved to the human perspective.

The Greeks grasped this problem when they sought to free up space in the mind. Being's boundlessness is an absolute idea. It refers to thinking that is allowed to give and take, modify or accommodate as a conversation proceeds. In practice this can only happen when mind empties of fixed positions and is able to respond to incoming thoughts. Only in this sense, as mind fills with being, does thinking become absolute. In other words, absolute means unfettered responsiveness to the world. By treating the absolute as a *process* of thinking the Greeks realised that unboundedness starts when the fixity of mind is challenged. The Greeks would agree we cannot access the world when we inhabit our own mind-bubble. But as an a priori the world is already here so, as we open the mind to it, our thinking begins to equate to the world, or *is* the world, if one wants to go that far.

Focusing on the way the mind works only allows us to describe the inside of the mind's bubble. This is why, as Kant pointed out, we see the world in terms of categories. These are the shadows on the cave wall that invite us to representation, narrative, signification or existence. We are little nearer than the poets of mythos to revealing the divinity that reflection was said to confer on mankind. Today there is only that which signifies - the text. All is mind; we have retreated from being. Post-structuralism misreads the Greek notion of the absolute.

We need to be clear what is entailed in the statement that the absolute is the only tool capable of returning human beings to the primordial world. The search involves the testing to destruction of a hypothesis by asking ever-bigger questions until all original suppositions have been abandoned or severely shaken and the discussion enters virgin territory. In other words, an absolute is not a claim to totality, a thing to be analysed, or an entity whose boundaries can be assayed. It involves a process that widens thinking without end. As the questioning process expands, the nature of the thinking about it changes. New, previously unconsidered possibilities arise, not only in the process of thinking but in being itself. Thoughts double back. A second thought reflects on a first. But a third thought's reflection on the second is a category step beyond the first reflection. So much has happened in between the two moves. Everything opens up, moves or expands. Thinking becomes less content-based or strictly logical and more open to meta-conceptual and intuitive processes. When this takes place in a group the interaction of participants can assume a higher level of non-specificity as fear of contradiction falls away. Questions and comments build on each other and thinking becomes more adventurous as intellectual exchange becomes dissociated from personality and self. Discussion becomes detached as conceptualisation proceeds afoot. Ideas attain to a profundity, unexpectedness or expansiveness unforeseen at the outset. These developments accrue as initial ideas are deconstructed and idiosyncratic or narcissistic viewpoints that arose during the discussion are abandoned. Only in this way can the bounds of extant thought be widened and overcome. 'Thinking at the absolute' might emerge only late in this process because the deconstruction of established viewpoints takes time and patience. A Platonic process of conceptualisation can now set consciousness free to return to being. The human claim to a 'mind of one's own' starts the process and is then gradually relinquished as discussion relaxes in the intellectual conviviality of the gathering. There is now room for opened-up minds to experiment with new relationships between mind and being.

An absolute makes allowance for all these considerations. The first thing we can say is that truth is hidden by the way we deal with human consciousness. Thus we are able to expand the context in which we live our lives when we let truth emerge. In this way we allow being full rein to intrude upon our mind. We can never fully 'grasp' truth by intellectual means alone. Truth-seeking is a process that one cannot know from the outside; that is to say, solely from the point of view of an enquiring mind.

These considerations explain the structure of this book. It started with the chipping-away of accretions of habit and inertia that prevent our minds from opening to manifestations of being. It then explored what emerges from within this exchange, conversation or dance between mind and being. Truth cannot be understood in any other way. To identify truth at the outset would be to resort to the dualistic thinking that has kept an understanding of truth at bay for thousands of years. Definition stultifies process. Process then collapses into old narratives; the resulting dissatisfaction is so uncomfortable that distraction is sought - whether in the form of sex, food, cultural minutiae, fascination with constructed activities like sport or politics, or many others. At this point many layers of defence will have been erected against truth. The whole point about truth is that it arises only when we let go of all certainties; not just opposites, but *all* positions.

The search for knowledge has diverted us into the shallow waters of theory. But absolute thinking is much more than this. It translates from early Greek as: 'to let a thing become itself.' It opens up thinking to a process of questioning that can lead us to the thing-in-itself, to the possibility that a state of irreducibility lies buried beneath the clutter of opinion, appearance and claims to knowledge or moral certitude. It must therefore be approached initially as a hypothesis to be tested, not as a statement or claim to be validated. Then, as Derrida has shown, it can loosen up knowledge-seeking thought to a process that dislocates and disturbs. As it moves away from certainty towards process it provides a more pliable, inclusive and expansive state of affairs within which to locate life than that offered by the analysis of knowledge. Opening up the hypothesis of the absolute allows more and more being to move to centre stage.

Process claims no authority for itself: it is complex, interactive, possessing feedback loops; it's impossible to pin down. It moves unpredictably, untouched by order and design. Its very indefinability creates a disturbance that serves to free thought, preventing it ossifying into opinion. Process lies beyond a point where 'selves' are constructed, where claims to possess a mind of one's own are vaunted. The latter produce only particularities and a fractured version of being.

The absolute is an idea of everything. Once we have given up searching for certainty it impinges on, indeed dishevels, mind. It is the thing-in-itself par excellence. Even more - it takes us into the realm of potentiality occupied by Bergson's duration, Nietzsche's eternal recurrence, Heidegger's unconcealment and Sartre's authenticity. Its universality cannot be traduced by the machinations of the mind. All attempts to address truth beyond correspondence and semantic theories accept that it is of the same order as being in a crucial sense - that it can only be accessed by thinking to the absolute (conceptualisation). Where the Greeks turned to absolutes to return them to source, isolated human beings now have to fall back on their own animation (or rather the agitation generated by their fear of natural animation) for a sense of substantiality. The classical concept of a source (or thing-in-itself), of something irreducible, was an a priori, a hypothesis about something already here waiting to be revealed. The phrase: *that it is* conveys the sense that it is prior to determination.

Today the focus is on *what it is*: a thing's composition, character or identity. But a source cannot be created to satisfy human exigencies such as will, desire or need. To create a source is an oxymoron. A copy can be made; a source *discovered*. A copy is a product of the human mind; a source originates in the world. Subjectivity is a creation, a copy and an unsatisfactory derivative that attempts to approximate to the source. The problem has been

131

around since classical times in the difference between essence and existence. Essence is the core or source of energy. It can provide energy to others. Existence derives its energy from another source; it is derivative and unstable. In an attempt to switch attention from the model building of German idealism to the human sphere Kierkegaard, Nietzsche and their followers created a phantom. Existentialism claims to be a core or thing-in-itself. But like subjectivity it lacks essence. In the eyes of the Greeks a claim to be a separate being by outward display carried little weight. This said little more than that we are separated by our skins. To the Greeks, an individual's openness to the world was the evidence of gravitas. Openness to the world was the first step in revealing oneself as a source. This move was clinched when one went further and opened to the truth of the world. This is why the absolute clears the way to a core that signifies equanimity towards the world.

The history of philosophy from Plato to post-structuralism keeps returning to the notion of the absolute. Thinkers have consistently approached it as if it is an idea that sits in the heavens as a state of perfection. It is not difficult to comprehend as an idea. Rather it seems impossible to comprehend as the ultimate ontology. The notion might not seem capable of addressing the problems that life throws up daily. The absolute might be said to tell us about the sublime that heaven confers. Yes, the sceptical observer might say, but we earthlings inhabit a riven world. Heraclitus' insight about nature or reality - that it presents itself in two aspects: the material and the immaterial - still has the power to dumbfound.

The absolute tells us about life in every unfolding moment. We *live* at the absolute. This is the point about the philosophical concept of the thing-in-itself. It is a notion about being free of mind. If I want to appreciate a painting I must first commit myself to looking at it without the intercession of my mind. Otherwise I will only take on board what my mind makes of the painting. I will entrench the current prejudices I hold. If I want to connect to it without mediation, so to speak, I must let it stand in its own right. My first move must be to release it from my subjective gaze. The mind no longer acts as my observer. Now I start to admit being directly into a cleared mind where it will affect me powerfully. And I cannot discount the possibility that I will affect the painting in its turn in some way. By looking at it without premeditation I can see the being the artist has brought to bear, way beyond the conventionalities of style or technique. Two entities - the painting and I - have connected directly because they are transparent to each other. Things can now occur beyond the bounds imposed by prior human knowledge. The space between the painting and I has been traversed by unmediated observation, a pure connection. Connectivity has become a thing-in-itself. Plato talked of reflection as human godliness. The process of thinking at the absolute takes us there.

Dare we now go further and postulate that neither mind nor being is fixed, that both possess untold potential? On one level, the world insists on presenting itself to us in the form of binaries, particularities and fragments. We can reconcile these disjunctions by conceptualising them. But at another level we are able to go further and mediate between the space opened up by this reconciliation and the in-itself. That is to say that the human dilemma arises from being in a mind-inflected world at the same time as being in a mind-free one. To open to such forces becomes possible only when we take mind and being to have no limits. In so doing we have removed all constraints on their spaciousness. Now we are able to do more than just test the limits of Platonic thought and to reconnect thinking to being. We have opened both to possibility. This requires us not merely to 'know' without seeking verification, substantiation or calibration, but to bring into play non-mind forces too.

In other words, we can recognise that it is we who are the problem for philosophy. As I pointed out in the Introduction, it is my perception of what it means to be human that stops me relating to you. And it is your attempt to be, based on your sense of a personal reality that prevents you relating to me. Yet, once we stop believing in human agency and put it into everything else, we are free. Philosophical friendship is the only friendship.

To reach this point something is required that we have not adduced so far, something that allows us to be at ease with indeterminacy. In the next chapter I identify this force as the muse.

CHAPTER TEN: TRUTH AS THE MUSE

'Tell us now, you Muses who have your homes on Olympos,

For you, who are goddesses, are there, and you know all things.'

Iliad, Book 2

As our clearing away of obstacles nears completion I am reminded of the way Socrates went about questioning certainty. He was called the wisest man in the world by the oracle. His wisdom lay in his ability to 'know' in an utterly different way from what we normally mean by knowing. For him knowledge involved connecting everything up, not separating everything out. In other words it was a matter of process and not the taking up of a position. The key figure he reached out to when this process hardened into positions was his muse Diotima. 'Socrates was subject to an auditory hallucination: a Divine Sign used to "speak" to him in warning when he was about to act amiss.' (1) She was a wise woman (according to the passage in the *Symposium*) who visited him in dreams or dazes, helping him to normalise the daily inconsistencies to which his mind was susceptible when overstretched.

We have unconcealed truth at last. Truth is the muse; Diotima is the true, hidden philosopher. She stands behind Socrates. Heraclitus reminded us that being (life at the source) unifies multiplicities. We do not need to add some momentous piece of wisdom. But what was required was that we got rid of the observer, the human vantage point. This means that when we listen to someone we can notice that they are both an identifiable person and an idea standing in for all of being external to us, at one and the same time. If I hold 'myself' back, everything outside me becomes active. This then serves to create me, but a more grounded me than the identity I have painfully tried to construct for myself over the years.

So, to return to the idea of a muse: I want to treat it playfully, in a nod to Plato's philosophical style. I have borrowed the idea from the Greek myths. There, the Muses are the daughters of Queen Memory. Their task is to take us back to the origin of things that has been lost to memory. Here, I want to change their role from that of memory-revivers to that of midwives of a *process of return*. This more dynamic usage is central to Plato's contention that we are already at the origin. By now it is becoming clear that we need more than merely to be reminded that we are real. This is because memory has not been lost, but rather covered up. We are left seeking a way to convert memory from the human-centred and structured thinking of narrative, excessive animation, Eros and goodness back into the fluid hurly-burly of life. A human initiative is needed to set the process of truth-seeking underway. This is where my use of the muse differs from that found in mythos or storytelling. Instead I will use it as a symbol of the Socratic questioning process or the disturbing of language and meaning to which Derrida alludes.

It is the final part of a process of release that allows the genie out of the bottle, freeing thought to roam. The muse-as-truth loosens up all knots to reveal the unity of all things. She helps us appreciate that nothing is incongruous whatever the situation, context or eventuality. Standing behind mind-thought-world, she *is* being, the real source or origin (or fulcrum) of the philosophical process. In a single sweep the clash between analytical philosophy/self/psychology on the one hand and classical or continental philosophy on the other is resolved. As being, the muse precedes the formation of the 'I,' breathing animation into philosophy and humanity at one and the same time.

Heraclitus' famous insight seems appropriate here. He said the world presents itself in two aspects - material and immaterial. We can add that the world also presents itself as both split and coherent. What has happened is that we have clutched at a sense of it being split, and have lost a sense of its coherence. We can now more fully appreciate the prescience of another of Heraclitus' insights - that all binary opposites are emergent unities. Can we entertain the possibility that, at one and the same time, being is both coherent and split - and that the capacity to entertain this possibility is the opening to truth?

I will approach this point by looking at three practical examples. The first is about a social science researcher who wants to see if art-for-itself can be helpful in therapy. At first the two activities seem drastically far apart because the concern is to apply art-for-itself (art centred on its own premises and practices) to therapy; not to make art a therapy in itself. The release into inter-relationship occurs when we let go of binary thinking. Once unimpeded thought sheds all sense of disparity between these two activities it flows freely. Freedom occurs when our thinking is no longer disposed to see as irreconcilable the relation of apparently disparate activities. Thinking that dissociates from fixed or pre-determined judgements and is open to all possibilities is truth. But its emergence doesn't rely solely on a decoupling of consciousness from binary thinking. Rather, it involves the opening to the fullness of consciousness. The muse allays forever any concern when faced with what at first glance appears to be a binary split. It rises above the very notion of binary thinking, of a split! Muse-truth is the capacity to see that all possibilities are forever open, however disjointed or disparate they may initially appear.

The break-through occurs in this very awareness. It is not a mind-construction but a limitless fluidity of thought. Barriers, categories and assumptions fall away. This is the point at which potential or hidden properties begin to emerge. The mind both returns to the world and is insightful about it at the same time. Now we can appreciate more fully the saying that philosophers *conceive* the truth with their minds and people *perceive* the truth around them. They occur at the same time. The truth-seeker sheds the encumbrance of clutter. This is not to say the truth-seeker is against societal clutter - he is beyond it. Philosophy disrupts everything, not in order to move to another instance, but to leave all instances behind and intact. Philosophy turns truth-seekers into close and alert observers of the world. Yet ironically it does this by extricating them from it. In this way, as Wittgenstein said, philosophy seeks to engage more fully with the world and not to change it.

The second example is about a friend who suddenly does something which shocks you; it is beyond all the reasonable expectations you entertained hitherto. It shatters your belief in him. Do you walk away? You can give yourself ample grounds for doing so. Or do you invoke the muse and shatter, not your belief in your friend, but *your judgements about him?* When you invoke the muse you become free to enter a more fluid space within which moral or epistemological fixities dissolve. This is the Platonic space where thinking attains to the absolute. You are starting to move beyond the moral imperatives and subjective shocks that drove your thinking to judge the situation. You begin to replace content with process. The content says that he definitely did what shocked you. The process involves asking, not whether or why he did that, but appreciating *that he did it*. We have now entered the realm of ontology and left epistemological description and judgement behind. Your friend, it is becoming clear, is not a grounded being but a conduit or channel of the thoughts and feelings of others. We are now able to move beyond personalities and start using being as a yardstick. Thus you can say that if he can do this then everyone can do this. The most interesting question of all now arises: why are human beings so affected by others? We have gone to the heart of philosophy.

The third example tells us something about the format of the philosophical canon. Nietzsche attacks Socrates mercilessly for his reliance on reason as an interrogatory tool in the *Dialogues*. At the same time Nietzsche promotes Dionysus as a visceral force that he believes is needed to counteract or overthrow reason. This seems to be a typical clash of philosophical opinion, a binary divide. Yet, on closer examination, we can see that both are vying for wholeness, Socrates by the use of *aporia* and Nietzsche by invoking Dionysus. Both seek fluidity of thinking - the absolute in Platonic terms - that will open the way forward. They seek a space that leaves room for everyone: the mad, criminal, poor, female, and those with skins deemed to be the wrong colour.

The dialectic is a final case in point. It starts from two positions and seeks to become one. But this is only as it seems. Both starting points, by virtue of being positions, are appearances. We can move from one to another *ad nauseam*. But the classic sense of the dialectic rises above both positions and leaves them intact, allowing us to be both in and above the apparent at the same time.

What has happened in all these cases is that we have liberated thinking from association with *both* subject *and* object. Gary Gutting says the postmodern attempt to do this has failed. Recent French thinkers have put the object into the subject and then all-but succeeded in abolishing the subject. But the subject obstinately refuses to die. Now we can see that subject and object are both mind-constructs, products of binary thinking. They can emerge as things-in-themselves, but this involves a lot of work. Nonetheless, people are now fully able to reconcile differences both within themselves and between them and others. People seem not to find great difficulty in reconciling their inner components. Accordingly, an inability to engage with another must involve a failure to 'dust off' the aspect of the self that finds an echo in the other. This will be achieved more successfully the more we throw ourselves fearlessly into the world, engaging with all and sundry and asking ourselves why we find X or Y difficult. With some work we can find X or Y's off-putting features inside us and learn to become reconciled to them. The effect is that freedom is within the reach of humankind. But in this process something else has happened too. We have released reflection back into being. Axial Age thinkers saw reflection as that which distinguishes human beings from other creatures. Thought has been liberated from the categories of subject and object to stay in mid-flight, so to speak. It had previously held thinker and idea in mutual suspension. Philosophy relieves both life and thought of impediment in Collingwood's words:

140

'Plato's contribution to the theory of philosophical method...is the conception of philosophy as the one sphere in which thought moves with perfect freedom, bound by no limitations except those which it imposes upon itself for the duration of a single argument...Consequently, thought ...is perfectly exemplified in that of philosophy; any one who thinks, and is determined to let nothing stop him from thinking, is a philosopher, and hence Plato is able to say that philosophy ...is the same as thought...' (2)

At last, the concepts of the third, the in-between, or God have found their true place within the world. Truth is movement, that which arises in the in-between. It is the All that harmonies all things. It is no longer a part of the unstable Greek harmony that tied it to goodness and beauty. Moreover, its place is now transparent. Persistent dualities such as subject vs object can now be put aside as primitive attempts to understand how human beings can engage with being. Even the epistemology-ontology divide is insufficient: truth is not confined by either concept. More otherness has yet to be incorporated. The more confident we are the more we can handle whatever the world throws at us. We can replace the established three moves in classical thinking that develop a full person (discover the one, relate it to the many, resolve the differences between the two) with a new three-part progression (at the top the muse, in the middle is Socrates of the opened-up mind who has been inspired by the muse, and at the bottom Socrates' interlocutor who stands for the world). It thus follows that we all need a Socrates in our life, not just to turn to for advice or to challenge our dichotomous thinking, but rather to act as a bridge or channel to our own Diotima or muse. Anthropomorphic hindrances wither away as binary opposites that have frozen into ice walls melt into water. Potential is released. Truth is process and movement; it is all.

CONCLUSION

'[Socrates] died in a calm, deliberate conviction, that Truth is really more precious than Life, and not only Truth but even the unsuccessful search for it.' Gilbert Murray, *A History of Ancient Greek Literature.*

We have arrived at truth to find that it is a process that enables us to be at ease with ourselves and with the world. Every thought can be reconciled within the whole, enabling all the dots to be joined up. Truth is the connectivity that releases human potential. It disturbs the forces that hold the ideas of mind and being in suspension and reconciles that space with a world that is not mind-determined. The outcome is a general loosening up that disturbs certainty and releases untold possibilities in all aspects of the whole. For sure we have not attained and are not seeking to understand being. Being just is. The aim of philosophy was set at the outset by Socrates. It is a human enterprise geared to releasing the 'human' from human bonds so that human beings can find their place in being. Philosophy examines the mind that relates to being in order to release people from the adverse effects caused by the workings of mind. Now thought can reach abstraction. This is human freedom. Truth can now be reconceptualised as the application of this abstraction to concreteness (the thing-in-itself). It is the unleashing of utterly liberated thought at the real-as-it-is. Truth is what happens when freedom encounters reality.

It matters not where we enter upon the task of discovering truth. All entry points converge and in so doing open other doors. Whether by taking thought to a meta-level or exploring the gap between mind and being; by shedding the temporary skin of narrative; by moving from love to agape; overcoming the panic that provokes an intensification of animation; or avoiding the compromised God-likeness of goodness, the choice of first move is irrelevant so long as a move is made. And making the first step calls on all our courage, which the Greeks possessed in abundance. Seeking *knowledge* of truth merely consigns us to the hall of mirrors that is epistemology. We are taking on a major, unending task, but one that is well within the capacity of human beings. It only matters that we start. This is because truth unites where other thought-systems cannot. Truth doesn't resort to bad habits or let extraneous elements seep in as it unites with being. It is a meta-regression that goes beyond this or that to everything, back to source or origin. It transcends both mind *and* being. A little of mind is preserved; we need not kill all theories. Mind offers a form of differentiation; we have to deal with this. Truth returns us nonetheless to thinking that is unmediated by mind - thinking that is pure becoming. It is where Heidegger sensed that physis (nature) and logos (thought) were held in productive tension. This is the state before Plato put such emphasis on mind.

Truth passes all the tests by developing further the Heraclitean insight that the world is all-inclusive. It is the play of harmony in the space of the in-between. Or, more radically still, it lies between entities where the only issues that arise worth concerning ourselves with are the natural needs of food, sleep, toilet and company. All else is a matter of choice over in-essentials. Emergence, immanence, excess: all are contained in this concept of truth. Our lives throw up innumerable challenges that distract us from being, but truth creates the space for being (and our thoughts) to come back together again - and then open to still further realms. I take it that Plato never wanted anything more than to continue the conversation or the dance between mind and being. By this I mean he never wanted an end to conversation, discourse or philosophical method. The pursuit of enquiry stood above all. He appreciated that thought not merely explains the universe; it incorporates us in it. He was of course right to seek to explain the process or tension that unites mind and being. His goodness-beauty-truth answer is in the end lacking. But, when we think about what he was aiming at, what he took to be overriding rather than what he actually said, then his preference for goodness is fully explicable. We might put his lapse into ethics and politics down to his love for Socrates and for want of any other reason attribute his addiction to instructional learning to his cerebral personality. None of this matters, for his grand idea rates alongside Thales' water, Democritus' atoms, Anaxagoras' nous, Aristotle's God or causes, Kant's reason and Hegel's dialectic. Plato's big idea was that mind is capable of reaching out to being and bringing all disparate things together.

We are always, even today, in danger of repeating his mistake of holding on to a single explanatory factor for too long. Too quickly thinkers identify causes for the direction and nature of philosophical thought. Presently language holds this prize. Who knows but truth may suffer this fate. But all great minds have sensed that here is a force that creates the bigger picture in which all fracturing is reconciled. However, when all is said and done, no mighty edifice, great system of thought or single-cause explanation can do the job that relentless enquiry does. After enquiry, everything pales as copies of copies.

Philosophy is a grand hypothesis. It has to do with enquiry. Someone says 'I am here and being is there.' Thought can then be used as a field that opens up possibilities in the intervening space. As our thinking loosens we realise we are the field; *we* are the flux. Postmodernism focuses on the parameters of this field, but there are none, other than at the level of appearance or simulacra. Postmodernism has thrown everything in the air - modernism, absolutes - the signified disappears in a receding line; ultra-scepticism reigns. All appears to be anti-Plato. Yet, Platonism never went beyond maintaining a conversation, method, pursuit or search. We need grand hypotheses like being, consciousness and truth. Indeed truth preceded Platonism. The movement is simple: one enters into a relationship with the world, takes advantage of reflection knowing that one is thereby creating a dualism but that this exercise is nonetheless useful. This kind of enquirer looks reality in the eye. Something happens as 'unconcealment' gets underway that promotes a developing relationship, an intensifying process, and a realisation that freedom beckons.

Truth is not like mind: it can't rationalise away being. It says in effect: being just is. If philosophy is to progress therefore we will have to pay a price if we stay in the human realm, keeping being at arm's length and equivocating over the mind-being gap. Alternately we can say that truth is, as far as we can see, a possibility that grows the more consciousness welcomes metaphysical questions. Here it reveals a monist universe that heals splits by viewing everything as an opening to a process of conceptualisation. Truth does not ignore people, but it is not about what we do together. Human affairs may or may not be sorted out between people. But truth is about the interplay of forces that configure the life we live as we relate to an indifferent world. It thereby raises fundamental questions like: who exactly are we?

A commitment to the joined-up-ness of any and all fragments does not force, seize upon or cut to shape incoming reality, or fall back on a selective approach in order to make things align. What happens is that when we view things from a fulcrum beyond the self all foregrounded issues become less pressing. We can take it that all our preoccupations are mind-constructions buoying up a sense of self. This is not a callous act: immediate issues find their place only when the perspective is grand. We cannot control ontology, whereas epistemological issues are manageable in common or garden terms. Neither does this exercise amount merely to a blurring of vision (although that might give temporary help). It is a true, potentially everlasting, commitment to intuition that does not exclude or rejig anything, but it does open to all possibilities, however outrageous they might first appear.

Truth is a meta-regression that goes beyond issues of this or that opinion, firstly to all opinions and to all minds, and then beyond them. It transcends both mind and being. Were we to get rid of mind there would not only be being left. Let us refer again to truth as the ontological *that it is* and mind to the epistemological *what it is*. They both seem to present themselves in our lives as obvious. Truth assays this gap. We will retain some mind so as not to be left with reality alone. Mind's dichotomising splits things into this *and* that. We have to deal with this by remembering that the difference between the parts does not constitute a split in the whole. Philosophy moves within the gap between mind and being *and* the in-itself, and it returns us to thinking before Plato. Here being is

147

unmediated by mind; thought is set free. Philosophy opens us up to becoming, to potential.

Truth reconciles opposites (and incongruities) - analytic and continental philosophy, self and world, truth and non-truth, truth as correspondence and truth as primordial. It is easy to bring Heraclitus and Parmenides together. Two ids are easier to bring together than two egos because they are not defended. We can reach beyond the apparent, the presented, to a place where Heraclitus and Parmenides meet. Indeed we mistake Plato if we dispute whether or not something lies beyond experience. This is just another binary quandary. Experience is fanciful and partial and yet it contains *something.* It is this something with which culture tantalises us. No, a dance takes place between philosophy and culture. It is the dance that matters. And the dance takes place where thought is boundless, at the absolute. John Caputo says we must see the absolute and relativity as extremes of thinking that must be avoided. But this is to miss the point of the Greeks. The absolute is not a stepping-stone to elsewhere, or an impossible step. There is *only* absolute - or metaphysical or universal - thinking. Perspectival thinking is human thinking, mind at work. All approaches to philosophy must be scrutinised to be sure that narcissism doesn't enter. That is to say we must always go beyond the mind's faculties.

Currently we only have the philosophy of the philosophers. This involves concealing being in constructs. When we treat being as if we can access it through the lens of intellectual constructs we are in danger of treating the people we are close to in an over-familiar, habituated way. And then we can find ourselves relating to a representation of them rather than to them themselves. We risk settling for constructions of ourselves. To break out of these structures we need to challenge the familiar and proximate. Otherness makes us think about that which underpins our claims to knowledge, to whatever is beyond mere association or being-with. But beyond otherness lies being. Will we make the extra effort and go there? There are ever more questions to ask and, like Odysseus, ever more resting places to leave behind. Philosophy thus has as its hallmark the duty to review itself as a move towards truth.

When we seek truth our lives will doubtless change because being reveals more of itself. Truth involves thinking about the other until the other appears differently. At this point the subject changes too. Only at this point does the other realise itself and become real. This plays out in daily life. For example, we can get our hands dirty: we need not fear the whiplash of conventional thought. Like Meursault in Camus' *L'Etranger* we can dare *not* to take on others' feelings. We can control an urge, for love or pity, to get actively involved in other's lives. Once we do this we see things anew: for example we can begin to appreciate that we are connected with the other person in myriad ways that pre-empt the social demonstration of connection. We may no longer feel the need to become over-involved. We can now slowly return to a world of formlessness, that is, to being. Being is not a seamless continuum. It is our minds that seek to comprehend it thus. We can hold back and not force things, and then watch the emergence of different clarities, feelings and nuances.

The Greeks gave a physical form to logos. They envisaged it playing out as a discussion about everything under the sun among all members of the community gathered in the open air of the public square. 'At least you can sense that they philosophised *differently* in Athens, above all in public. Nothing is less Greek than the conceptual cobwebbery of a hermit,' is Nietzsche's teasing view. (1) Their political thought set the interests of community or polis above those of the individual. Before the rise of philosophy everyone was one of the Many. Philosophy drew them into the One. Socrates was concerned with developing personal character to this end. Only in late Plato is an urgent concern with society revealed. The question both Socrates and Plato asked was: how do we incorporate the many into the one without loss of freedom? The answer lay in their participatory community and democracy where everyone was expected to give a reasoned and nuanced (or shouted, if not otherwise possible) *public* expression of their logos. They realised that freedom of one is freedom of many. Each individual is one and many (guardian and people). Only when individuals are at ease with what it means to be a 'one,' and can let that one sally forth, can they form into a society that is a larger replication of the individual.

Knowing that the individual mind is prone to illusion and that we have nothing else with which to start a discussion, they flocked to the public square and amphitheatre to give and hear views that shattered the illusions in their minds. What they encountered was not always to their liking. Their own views might not have been treated with the approbation they desired. But they could take the heat. They called the muse-truth into being. As a result more being beckoned. With other interactive members of the community they turned to being as a touchstone. Infelicities of mind melted away in the heat of this furnace. Relations were direct; obscurities were laid bare. 'Idiotes' - a private citizen - was someone who was ignorant and isolated from public affairs, as Pericles attests: 'We are unique in considering the man who takes no part in public affairs, not to be apolitical, but useless.' ((2) No-one was odd or felt left out. If someone felt he misunderstood he would ask others: 'what happened there?' If he was not invited to a party he would assume others weren't either. People spoke as 'we,' not 'I.' All life was public and interactive - or inter-subjective, to use a recent term.

Today discourse and public life are profoundly anti-Greek. Agitated isolation abounds amid mass exhortation. A big gap exists between the' I' or self and the mass. But beyond the hubris of the lonely battling hero we can discern the possibility of an emergent friendship in which both mutual acceptance and straight talking have their place; in a word, agape. Truth-seeking takes us beyond life as a coping exercise ('fight or flight') where everything stops short, where life is treated as if every move will meet resistance. Freud saw the id as unstable. He gave the ego the job of monitoring its relation to the critical public voice of the superego. He was saying we can do no more than temporise and moderate. But the search for truth doesn't stop there. It asks: why live in a shadow land? Truth is what emerges as we take the heat, reveal our id in all its natural exuberance, articulate our own thoughts and let others' thoughts in. By taking our 'self' into the public square we can start opening up to the world. We can begin to accept we don't need redemption because we have done no wrong. Awful pain may characterise the world but, though one feels much of it, one doesn't need to take personal responsibility for it all. If we feel lonely we can join other truth-seekers whom society has docketed as psychological index patients. Like them we begin to realise that stepping away from family, culture, tribe and nation is just a first move in our search for truth.

The Greeks located all obstacles to truth in domestic or familial life. Accordingly Socrates took upon himself the task of being the midwife of public life, in effect, by freeing people from constraints so they can be fully paid up participants in the public arena. He realised that public life was untenable until each individual was whole and free and able to hold his own in public. Freud told us that all of life subsequent to birth is about separation (not joining up, as today's society enjoins us). We start life in a union with mother. But in order to know ourselves we must separate. Only then will we stop romanticising about others and instead start to relate to them wholeheartedly. When we move from erotic love to agape, from mind to being, from narrative to absence of story, when we make the move from knowing only those who are easy to be with (domestic, professional, social, neighbourhood) to those who stretch us and take us into unknown territory, only then will we have encountered the universality of the public square. In so doing we bring together what our gaze has settled on and what our gaze has missed out. This is what it means to move from the love story of the family to a friendship with everyone in the public square.

The Greek public square originally operated according to the rules of family life. Each member was in thrall to the familiar and protected against the profound and unexpected. Socrates chipped away at the power of roles and other defences in the domestic and work life of his interlocutors in order to discover the hidden real person. He then released this mature human being into the public square. In effect Socrates *created* the public square. If he had not reached out to the person behind the appearance real people would never have been born! Now at last it is becoming clear that the public square is logos; logos is agape; agape is being, and that providing access to them all is truth. All point in the same direction, towards a society open to potentiality, to new ideas. Equally, all the impediments to the emergence of truth - narrative, excessive animation, erotic love and goodness - are products of or contribute to an over-active mind. The public square is where the newly born of the world meet to work out new rules of engagement suitable for free persons. The hold of the regulated domestic arena over communal gatherings is broken at last.

The same idea applies to a conversation. It can be said that six people take part in a conversation - the two conversationalists and the parents of the two. We could go further and say the parents' parents are present as well. When we let our minds regress infinitely we realise the whole world is present in the conversation. In this case it is impossible to know who is speaking and who listening. A point made by A triggers a response in B that is associated with someone way back in B's family hinterland. B's response throws A off-course: it does not seem to come from the person they know. The conversation begins to jump around like a ball in a pin-board game, as different parts of the family hinterland are drawn in. The whole world starts chipping in as the interconnections expand and regress. When we let go of our control over a conversation it quickly moves beyond the superficial and premeditated. The terms 'speaker' and 'listener' are misnomers. Subjectivity gives way to inter-subjectivity, division to wholeness. We can extend this idea to Socrates and his interlocutor. Their conversation appears to be a one-on-one encounter. But if we insert the muse above Socrates, with the task of universalising his errant thoughts, and below him place the family and social hinterland of his interlocutor, we see how the figure of Socrates is a bridge between teeming populations. What

Socrates has done is to unblock what might otherwise have been a stultifying, superficial conversation between two people who perceived themselves merely as two identities. Socrates is the channel that allows all these people to communicate. Socrates *is* the public square.

Philosophy is a baby. It has many enemies, even inside. It is fragile and easily converted into linguistics, science and psychology. The latter lack the spirit of philosophy because their thinking is either binary or anthropomorphic. They focus on human frailty. But the present exploration has taken the route of Continental philosophy which foregrounds universality, movement and being. Here there is no need of a relationship between opposites; I do not see the other in the mirror; or become another to myself. We do not even have to try and get opposites to agree in the form of corroboration, or to verify the in-between by substantiation. Certainly, thought easily splits. Who is to say whether or not this will be shown to be the case with being? It is nonetheless the case that everyone is correct; there are no wrong ideas. All that is needed is that the *conversation never ends,* that we keep listening to the other, we never stop the movement, the dance, we don't ever settle on an outcome, opinion, or verdict. All opinions are merely aspects of process that have ossified into dichotomies. Philosophy offers us many ways to handle them. Truth provides this space. Truth-seeking is philosophy.

END NOTES

INTRODUCTION

(1) I refer to being, reality, world and universe interchangeably hereafter. These are not references to this planet. I evolve a workable, new definition of being in Chapter Two and believe this can adequately be related to reality as a concept of everything there is, always keeping in mind that being involves human reflection and is much more complex, layered and nuanced than the stark, bright and harsh 'thereness' and 'hereness' of reality.

(2) The other two provinces are knowledge as epistemology and virtue as ethics.

(3) Franz Rosenzweig, *The Star of Redemption* (Madison, University of Wisconsin Press, 2005) p 408.

(4) Martin Heidegger, *Basic Writings* (London, Routledge and Kegan Paul, 1978) Parts II and III.

(5) Iris Murdoch, *The Fire and the Sun: Why Plato Banished the Artists* (Oxford, Clarendon Press, 1977) p 60.

(6) John D Caputo, *Truth: The Search for Wisdom in the Postmodern Age* (London, Penguin, 2016); Simon Blackburn, *Truth: A Guide for the Perplexed* (London, Penguin, 2006).

CHAPTER THREE: RELEASING TRUTH FROM BONDAGE

(1) The arguments in support of goodness are laid out in Iris Murdoch, *Existentialists and Mystics; Writings on Philosophy and Literature* (ed. Peter Conradi) (New York, Penguin, 1998).

CONCLUSION TO SECTION ONE

(1) Iris Murdoch, *The Sovereignty of Good,* (London, Routledge and Kegan Paul, 1970) p 95.

CHAPTER FIVE: THE GAP BETWEEN MIND AND BEING

(1) Gilbert Murray, *Hellenism and the Modern World* (London, George Allen and Unwin, 1953) p 35.

(2) RG Collingwood, *An Essay on Philosophical Method* (Oxford, The Clarendon Press, 1933) p 15.

(3) Rosenzweig, *Star of Redemption,* p 414.

(4) Heidegger, *Basic Writings*, p 120.

CHAPTER SIX: NARRATIVE

(1) Plato, *The Republic,* Book 10.

(2) Roberto Calasso, *The Marriage of Cadmus and Harmony* (New York, Knopf, 1993) p 390.

(3) Private communication from George Dimitri.

(4) Collingwood, *Philosophical Method*, p 214.

(5) Walter Pater the 19th century aesthetic critic wrote: 'For in truth all art does but consist in the removal of surplusage, from the last finish of the gem-engineer blowing away the last particle of invisible dust, back to the divination of the finished work to be, lying somewhere, according to Michelangelo's fancy, in the rough-hewn block of stone.' Quoted in Elizabeth Prettejohn, 'Surplusage!' *London Review of Books* (Vol 42, No 3, 6 February 2020).

(6) Fredric Jameson, 'In Soviet Arcadia,' *New Left Review* (75, May-June 2012).

CHAPTER EIGHT: EROS

(1) Alain Badiou [with Nicolas Truong], *In Praise of Love* (London, Serpent's Tail, 2012) p 99.

CHAPTER NINE: CONCEPTUALISATION

(1) Friedrich Nietzsche, *The Will to Power,* 552, quoted in William McNeill and Karen S Feldman (eds) *Continental Philosophy* (Blackwell, Malden MA, 1998) p 87.

.

CHAPTER TEN: TRUTH AS THE MUSE

(1) Gilbert Murray, *A History of Ancient Greek Literature* (New York and London, D Appleton, 1916, facsimile copy) p 173.

(2) Collingwood, *Philosophical Method*, p 15.

CONCLUSION

(1) Friedrich Nietzsche, *Twilight of the Idols* (New York, Oxford University Press, 1998) p 54.

(2) Alev Scott, 'Britons should learn to vote like the Ancient Greeks,' *Financial Times*, 25 November 2019.

SELECT BIBLIOGRAPHY

Michael James Bennett, 'Deleuze and Heidegger on Truth and Science,' *Open Philosophy* (Vol 1, Issue 1, 20 December 2017).

John D Caputo, *Truth: The Search for Wisdom in the Postmodern Age* (London, Penguin. 2016).

Martin Heidegger, *Basic Writings* (Ed. David Farrell Krell) (Abingdon, Routledge and Kegan Paul, 2011), Parts II and III.

Karl Popper, 'On the Sources of Knowledge and Ignorance,' *Encounter* (Vol XIX, No 3, September 1962).

Jean-Paul Sartre, *Truth and Existence* (Chicago, University of Chicago Press, 1995 edition).

Vladislav Suvak, The Essence of Truth *(Aletheia)* in the Western Tradition in the Thought of Heidegger and Patocka in *Thinking Fundamentals,* 1WM, Junior Visiting Fellows Conference, Vol 9/4, Vienna, 2000.

Jan Wolenski, 'Aletheia in Greek Thought until Aristotle,' *Annals of Pure and Applied Logic,* 127 (2004) pp 339-360.

GLOSSARY

ABSOLUTE (THE) is a concept with theological connotations. It conveys that which is not bounded by or conditional on anything else. It is a meta regression to origin. It can stand for the ground of being or the unity of reality.

A PRIORI (AN) is a supposition about a state of being that subsists before thought is brought to bear on it. It makes necessary that the thinker acknowledges the always-already nature of reality and the subjective nature of mind.

FULCRUM is another term for metaphysics. It derives from Archimedes' claim that that if one finds ground firm enough and a piece of wood long enough to rest on a fulcrum, a small object at one end could balance the world at the other. This analogy conveys a sense that the world can be comprehended by conceptualising it. It says that, by stepping far enough away from the world in thought, one encompasses the whole.

METAPHYSICS is a form of enquiry that asks about the nature of things. As such it grounds philosophical thinking and underpins all branches of philosophy.

MIND (THE) is a concept of the structuring capacity of cognitive powers. By imposing definition and order on thought it blocks thought's free movement. It is not a capacity inherent in the world. It arises out of a human predilection for thought to be made personal and subjective. Mind can be made innocuous once it is anchored in the body, that is to say, in the world.

OTHER (THE) is a concept associated with Emmanuel Levinas. He claimed that the Other stands outside a self's mental construction of the world. Whether as an actual person or something that is beyond rational recognition, the Other breaks through the categories of thought that govern the way one lives. Levinas insists that the Other is crucial for one to be a person, both as a moral agent and as a reflective, rational being.

PROCESS occurs when the movement of thought is unimpeded such for example as when the mind is prevented from imposing structures on thinking or diverting thought to considerations of content.

REALITY is a concept of everything that there is. It can contain internal dualities without itself being split.

SOCIO (THE) or SOCIAL is a term used by Deleuze to explain being in terms of human aggregation. It denotes a force that is implicit in the coming together of human beings that reconciles the flux of thought and the placidity of being (as nature).

THOUGHT arises out of the reflective capacity inherent in the world. Its freedom of movement is preserved when it is not constrained by the mind expressing itself in the form of a self.

BIOGRAPHICAL NOTE

Roy Sturgess has taught economic history in universities in England, Scotland and the United States and has been a research associate in Palestine. He took up philosophy in retirement and continues to participate in groups that explore philosophy as a conversation, a Socratic dialogue or as a process.

INDEX